Dina Saalisi

The ART of
FLOWER
THERAPY

A Comprehensive Guide to Using the
Energy of Flowers to Heal, Thrive, and
Live a Vibrant Life

REDFeather™
MIND | BODY | SPIRIT

4880 Lower Valley Road, Atglen, PA 19310

Library of Congress Control Number: 2023931163

Cover & design by Danielle D. Farmer
All images curated by Dina Saalisi, licensed from Deposit Photo except for image 01-02, taken by Lane Eib, and images 02-24, 03-01, 03-02, 03-03, 03-04, taken by David Saalisi.
Photo by Evie Shaffer: https://www.pexels.com/photo/pink-grey-and-white-petaled-flowers-clip-art-2395251, Photo by Evie Shaffer: https://www.pexels.com/photo/white-flower-2512387, Photo by NEOSiAM 2021: https://www.pexels.com/photo/white-dandelion-flowers-595102/
Type set in Priori Serif OT/Kudryashev Display/Priori Sans OT

ISBN: 978-0-7643-6697-0
Printed in China

Published by REDFeather Mind, Body, Spirit
An imprint of Schiffer Publishing, Ltd.
4880 Lower Valley Road
Atglen, PA 19310
Phone: (610) 593-1777; Fax: (610) 593-2002
Email: info@redfeathermbs.com
Web: www.redfeathermbs.com

FSC.org
MIX
Paper | Supporting responsible forestry
FSC™ C104723

For our complete selection of fine books on this and related subjects, please visit our website at www.redfeathermbs.com. You may also write for a free catalog.

REDFeather Mind, Body, Spirit's titles are available at special discounts for bulk purchases for sales promotions or premiums. Special editions, including personalized covers, corporate imprints, and excerpts, can be created in large quantities for special needs. For more information, contact the publisher.

We are always looking for people to write books on new and related subjects. If you have an idea for a book, please contact us at proposals@schifferbooks.com.

For Mom

Contents

PREFACE

The people and events described in this book are based on my work as a Bach Foundation Registered Practitioner and a National Board Health and Wellness Coach. The names of my clients, students, and colleagues have been changed to protect their privacy. The case studies came from my privilege of witnessing the candid stories of others, lending a compassionate ear, and offering gentle support for their healing.

ACKNOWLEDGMENTS

I'm immensely grateful for each of my teachers, clients, and students who shared their wisdom and courage with me to make this work possible; Dr. Edward Bach for his visionary awareness of subtle energy medicine; my family, whose love and support I cherish; and for the flowers that continually spread their light.

INTRODUCTION

My earliest experience of flower remedies as a powerful healing ally was in my midtwenties, with the birth of my son. After three days of difficult labor and an intense birth, we were both exhausted and in shock. Our family doctor, a naturopath, recommended I try Rescue Remedy® to soothe the feelings of birth trauma. I clearly recall taking the remedy and putting a drop on my son's lips before nursing one night. After days of relentless crying (both of us), we gently dozed into a deep sleep. I continued to use Rescue Remedy® for about a week afterward, and I felt the energy of the flowers offering both of us strength and fortitude. I was sold!

I dove in and read every book I could get my hands on about the Bach flowers, and I began to understand how they worked on a deep, energetic level. I had been studying Western herbal medicine for many years, and this deeper understanding of how our emotions govern our physical bodies offered a next step in honing my skills in holistic healing. I wholeheartedly embraced the art of flower therapy, using the essence of flowers as a catalyst to heal myself. I decided to address the challenging emotions I was experiencing as a new mother—I was anxious, irritable, and impatient. I bought a bottle of impatiens, and as I took the remedy over the course of a few weeks, I felt an expansive sense of calmness. This was a relief, and it felt so good that I began to see my emotions in a new light. After much soul-searching, I realized that from early on I had been taught to ignore my feelings and "just get over it." Through this new lens of flower energy, I was able to tap into and honor the "negative" feelings I was experiencing, which brought a new sense of clarity and balance into my life.

Flower therapy was asking me to listen to my inner voice and reflect on what was calling to be heard, and ultimately to be healed. I liked this new way of experiencing my emotions, and I was ready to explore the next layer of healing. Upon deeper reflection, I remembered that ever since I was a small child, I was often fearful of many things, which made me appear timid and shy. I was the girl at the party who would sit on the sofa and wish I were invisible, while everyone else danced and had fun. Painfully, I recalled the feelings of awkwardness and fear. Now, I could see how this pattern still surfaced and how it held me back from a deeper connection with others and with life. For a few months I worked with mimulus remedy, and I recall the gradual shift toward feeling courageous and supported. My ability to speak up and explore new things, without fear, was strengthened, for the first time in my life.

Many years later, after the entertainment production business my husband and I owned and operated had closed, I developed a severe, blistering rash on both of my hands and shins. It was something I had never experienced before, and I struggled with trying to find a cure. I saw several doctors who couldn't offer me a diagnosis or treatment. My daily rhythm was derailed, since I was unable to do even basic household chores. I focused on how bad I felt, and I wallowed in a negative state of self-pity for many months. Eventually, after trying everything from dietary changes to pharmaceutical drugs, I realized that the root cause of my health problem was indeed related to my emotional state.

I began to select flower remedies on the basis of my varying emotions throughout the illness. As I took the time to tune into my deeper feelings, I recognized that I was depressed over the loss of our business and had lost my motivation and desire to do anything. I used wild rose for a few weeks, which reconnected me to life and gave me strength to forge ahead and continue through the various layers of my healing. In this downturn I was reunited with the profound healing of flowers, and I wanted to take my learning to the next level. Synchronistically, I found a six-week flower therapy class that was starting the following month, and I joined. Little did I know at the time that this class would lead me in the direction of pursuing meaningful work. As I immersed myself in the world of flowers, my skin steadily began to heal. As I was led by a passionate call, my perspectives shifted, and I saw my physical challenge as an opportunity to learn and grow. My old business had failed, yet what a gift it was to return to my first love of the healing arts, with renewed vigor, and to lead others along the path of healing with flowers.

As a holistic healer, I witness others who suffer with various physical and emotional challenges. Often, they seek me out as a last-ditch effort to address issues that mainstream medicine hasn't been able to effectively support. I always start by encouraging them to become more aware of and voice their emotions, without shame, and to embrace a sense of loving acceptance for everything they are experiencing, especially that which is difficult. To be able to work from a place of our core challenges is where the deepest healing occurs. This is the first and most important step in flower therapy—to touch our shadows with honesty and hold our challenges with tenderness, so that we can bestow the transformative, light-filled energy of the flowers upon ourselves.

Over the years, I've gotten to know each of the thirty-eight Bach flower remedies as potent allies given to us by nature. This self-healing system is meant to be simple, easy to use, and effective. This book is my offering, to inspire others to communicate with the flowers, listen to their songs, and embrace the healing of this energetic resonance. Through the lens of flower therapy, my hope is that you too will realize that suffering is an invitation to look within, and to view emotional challenges in ways that support new awareness, continued growth, and innate healing.

CHAPTER 1
Nature Heals

The dawn of a new and better art of healing is upon us.

—Edward Bach

What Are Flower Remedies?

Ever since the beginning of time, everywhere in the world, wildflowers have been used as medicine. The flowers found in roadside ditches, riverbeds, and meadows, the ones we call weeds, are the most powerful. They grow where no person has planted them, and the birds, bees, and animals are their gardeners. Vibrant colors and sweet fragrances that naturally occur hold a quality that goes beyond reason and reaches deep within our souls. Although we can quantify, measure, and try to make sense of the ways in which nature operates, there is still a great mystery that goes beyond what can be calculated or seen. Within this liminal space, everything is connected, and the vibrational energies affect one another in an invisible yet felt way. As the energy fields of humans and flowers join, they produce a resonance that can be attuned to and ingested in the form of the energy, or "essence," of the flower.

In 1930s England, renowned physician, bacteriologist, and homeopath Dr. Edward Bach developed a system of using flower remedies to relieve the disharmony of disease. He felt strongly that there was a simple method of medicine that would allow for the mind, body, and soul connection of each individual person, without placing an emphasis on physical symptoms. He was a pioneer in his field and, without the support of the medical community, left behind a successful practice and immersed himself in nature in search of a psycho-spiritual self-help system. Through keen intuition, clever insights, and deliberate trials, he was led to discover that his own challenging emotions could be balanced with the positive, energetic qualities from 38 select flowers. He captured the "essence" of each flower by floating the freshest blooms in a glass bowl of spring water, activated by the sun or by boiling in a pot over a stove. He tested the remedies by taking them internally for several weeks at a time, and he recognized a shift in consciousness and a sense of renewed equilibrium. He was an intuitive and an empath and could feel the positive effects of the flowers on his negative emotional states. He began offering the remedies to his patients, which further affirmed their effectiveness. By the end of his life, he was certain of his simple system of healing with thirty-eight distinct flowers. Flash-forward nearly ninety years later. Holistic healers all over the planet have taken up Dr. Bach's call to guide others to "heal thyself." There are over three hundred flower essence makers throughout the world, who've developed remedies for nearly every flower. Flower remedies are sold in over sixty countries and used for self-care, as well as by healing arts professionals as a complementary therapy for deeper emotional-healing work.

This book focuses on the original thirty-eight Bach flower remedies. My intention is for it to be used as a guide on how to deeply attune to the psycho-spiritual dimensions of nature, and to gain a solid foundation to explore the healing attributes of flower remedies. Do I work with other flower remedies outside the Bach system? I believe that every flower, plant, rock, and animal has energy that we as humans can intentionally attune to. As a flower therapy educator, I feel that to achieve the best results in working with the energy of flowers is to begin with and get proficient at understanding the emotional challenges displayed in the thirty-eight Bach flowers and expand from there. In my practice I incorporate other flower and gem remedies, but only after clients and students have had success with the Bach flowers for some time.

There is no true healing unless there is a change in outlook, peace of mind, and inner happiness.

—Edward Bach

How to Work with Flower Energy

Flower energy is all around us, and it's here to stay. Often when I'm working with someone to support their healing process, nature is noted as a foundational element for well-being. I've yet to find anyone who doesn't feel more alert, alive, and inspired while outdoors. Even in cities we can find respite in parks, gardens, or our own backyard. So, when we talk about working with the energy from flowers, we're talking about a connection with the greater world around us. We are part of this universal sphere, which governs every living being on the planet. It's no wonder we feel at ease when we give in to the phenomenon of nature. The art of flower therapy starts by recognizing nature as the greatest teacher and by taking time each day to physically connect with this source of nourishment. Once we feel held in this way, we can then begin to discover what holds us back from healing our wounds.

Flower therapy asks us to notice our emotional state and to recognize what feels most challenging. This is a deep process of going inward and reflecting on our sorrow, fear, and anger with honesty and compassion. It is a profound method of self-care, which not only gives us what we need to gently heal, but also connects us to our souls by way of deeper awareness. When we learn how to name our challenging emotional states without shame, then we can choose to tune into the energy of the flowers to transform the imbalance. It's a beautiful process of self-discovery that allows for authenticity and positive change.

Years ago, I met with a young woman who was suffering with a complex, chronic, undiagnosed illness. She was sick for over three years and had seen over one hundred healthcare professionals, everyone from psychics to surgeons. When we met for the first time, I listened to the harrowing accounts, then responded simply by asking, "How does all of this make you feel?" With tears, she said that I was the first one to ask her this question. I was shocked by this omission from the various practitioners, and my client's touching reaction made me more aware of how the power of pausing and recognizing what one is experiencing emotionally is of vital importance in catalyzing the healing process.

The first rule of flower therapy is to treat the person, not the disease. To select remedies on the basis of the current emotional picture of the individual—*never on the symptoms*. While it's true that different people will experience the same type of illness in varying ways, mainstream medicine still prescribes on the basis of physical symptoms, without focusing on how a person *feels*. Decades of research has shown that the emotions indeed govern the body, and so the inner landscape is where we travel to discover how to truly heal. In working with flower energy, we must become aware of the emotional challenge, recognize the ways in which each person reacts differently, and utilize the corresponding remedies. This goes against the medical model of diagnoses, since it focuses on the unique response to illness that each individual person has, rather than the physical markers of pain. Instead of "Where does it hurt?," the question becomes "How does this illness make you feel?"

Dr. Bach recognized human emotion as the key component in holistically healing the body, mind, and soul. When he developed the flower remedy system, he grouped the thirty-eight flowers into seven categories of emotional challenge that he deemed responsible for holding one back from healing. Fear, uncertainty, insufficient interest, loneliness, oversensitivity, despair, and overcare all are seen as universal emotional challenges that can be confronted and transformed. When I teach students how to use flower remedies, I always start with Dr. Bach's categories. I find it easier to reflect on emotions, when we have a starting point that narrows it down, rather than sifting through all thirty-eight flower indications to find the best allies. When you first start to select remedies for yourself, you may feel like you need all the flowers at once! Indeed, we have all experienced the various emotional descriptions of each flower, at one time or another in our lives. As you learn the indications for each flower more intimately, you begin to realize that there are a few flowers that feel particularly "special" to you, and that relate to your own personal challenges. I find that the provocations that relate to my particular set of flowers occur less often as my awareness of these challenges grows. For instance, my whole life I've been a quick thinker and move ahead of others to get things done. Early on in my flower therapy studies, I identified impatiens as a relatable remedy and used it over a period of time to receive the benefits of calmness and patience. My nature is still to be quick, yet now when I notice a sped-up, anxious state, I can simply remind myself to slow down, and this awareness is enough to receive the healing energy of impatiens.

One way to start working with flower energy is to recognize which flowers feel most relevant to your habits, patterns, and challenges and to take the single remedy of a particular flower for a month or two, until you notice a softening of your edges. From here you will be in a receptive state to work on the next layer that arises. As you resolve each challenge, what was below the surface comes to the fore, and you are presented with your next opportunity for growth. The cycle continues, as do life's challenges, and each time you become better able to handle the stressors. Flower therapy is an ongoing, self-reflective process. An inward journey that leads you toward new awareness of your emotions, feelings, and sensations—there is no finish line, but a willingness to continually reflect on your experiences with curiosity and care.

Taking moments regularly to recognize your emotional state helps you choose remedies for yourself with clarity and ease. It's a process of getting to know yourself on a deeper level, which allows for the healing to be catalyzed from within. The next step in recognizing your emotional state is to decipher if what's arising is chronic or acute. Sometimes you don't even realize you've been plagued by a continual feeling of anger, grief, shame, or fear until you've paused to reflect on the patterns.

Practice

Reflecting on My Emotional State

Sit quietly with your eyes closed and take five deep, cleansing breaths.

Once you feel relaxed, ask yourself in your mind's voice: *"What am I feeling in this moment?" "Where do I feel it in my body?"* Allow the first answers that arise to be your truth.

Breathe a little more deeply into the areas of your body that are holding the emotions.

Slowly open your eyes. Take a few minutes to write about this experience.

Are the emotions you're experiencing chronic or acute?

What flowers might you offer yourself? (Use chapter 2 to read about the different flower indications.)

Journaling is a foundational way to become familiar with your emotional landscape and helps illuminate the messages from your unconscious mind that are hard to access otherwise. I use "stream of consciousness" writing every morning as a form of emotional hygiene and to connect with what's below the surface.

Practice

Listening to My Inner Voice

First thing in the morning, put pen to paper (not hands to keyboard) and just write. You can set a timer for ten minutes or fill two or three pages. The idea is to let your unconscious mind do the work, without editing or overthinking.

Recording any dreams from the night before, in as much detail as possible, is a wonderful way to deepen the process.

At the end of the session, put your journal away, then repeat the practice each morning.

On the new and full moon of each month, reread your writings to observe any patterns or insights. Guaranteed there will be many.

How to Create a Combination Flower Remedy

When working with flower remedies, you are the alchemist. In the "Resources" section at the end of this book, you will find where to purchase single flower remedies (stock bottles). You can buy a complete set of the thirty-eight Bach remedies, or you can buy single remedies as you need them. I recommend getting a complete set so that you can start formulating right away. A 10 mL stock bottle remedy contains over two hundred drops. When you mix a formula, you need only two drops of each flower, so stock bottles last an incredibly long time. And yes, it's true that only two drops of a single flower remedy are enough to contribute their healing energy to a mixture. Creating a combination formula for yourself, and for others, is a nourishing practice that can be done monthly. As you pause to reflect on what you're currently experiencing, you connect with your challenges and recognize them as the fuel needed for transformation. And what better catalyst than flowers!

The rule of thumb is to mix two to seven flowers in a combination formula to address the various facets of the emotional challenges experienced. Why no more than seven? My sense is that when we're able to refine the number of flowers chosen, we take the "less is more" approach and arrive at the most necessary and potent combination possible. I start by jotting down all the flowers that correspond to the challenges, then I narrow it down from there. I might begin with a questionable dozen or more, and upon deeper consideration I usually arrive at a certain five or six that are the most relevant, *at the current time*. This is an important point—never select remedies on the basis of past feelings. You can ask yourself (or whomever you're working with), *What am I (are you) currently feeling?* It can be helpful if you close your eyes or lower your gaze to reflect inwardly. Remember, this is not about how the physical symptoms affect your body, but how it feels on the inside when you're faced with physical limitations.

Use a 1 oz. dropper bottle filled three-quarters full with spring water.

Add two to three droppersful or about 1 teaspoon of alcohol spirits as a preservative. Grape brandy is traditional, but any drinking alcohol will do. For children and those avoiding alcohol, you can use apple cider vinegar or vegetable glycerin.

Add two drops of each flower remedy directly from the stock bottle to the dropper bottle of preserved spring water.

Once you've added up to seven flowers, you'll have a combination flower remedy dosage bottle.

Write the date on the bottle and the combination of flowers used. It's a good idea to keep either written or electronic notes of the formula for future review.

How to Take a Combination Flower Remedy

Place four drops from your dosage bottle, directly on your tongue, four times daily: upon waking, before going to sleep, and twice in between. When it comes to dosage, more is better than less. When you begin a new remedy, you can take more than four doses, the first few days, to catalyze the healing energies.

Alternatively, you may add several drops to a glass of water or your water bottle and sip throughout the day, for four doses.

For very young children, babies, and anyone who wishes to use the remedies topically, you can use a 1 oz. spray bottle and apply four sprays, four times daily, to pulse points, the top of the head, or the soles of the feet.

Your bottle should last about three to four weeks.

Typically the emotional shift is gradual, with a sense of renewed balance over this course of time.

Upon taking a new remedy, you may become more aware of your challenging emotional state, which may feel like a worsening of symptoms. This is indeed confirmation that the remedies are working, since the flowers do not enhance our negative states but shed light on the shadows emerging from within. This should subside within a day or two. In the meantime, you can back off the dosage and take Rescue Remedy®, until you feel rebalanced.

Flower remedies do not interfere with other healing modalities, herbs, or medications.

A Note on Dosage

As with any practice that yields benefits, consistency is the key. Dosage is always two drops of a single flower remedy or four drops of a combination formula.

For acute treatment of sudden emotional states, place two drops of a single flower remedy directly from the stock bottle onto your tongue or, alternately, put two drops in a glass of water and sip. Repeat at least four times a day, for as much as is needed. If there is no felt shift after two days of use, it may not be the right remedy, or perhaps the emotional state is more deeply rooted than thought. Dig a bit deeper to reevaluate your feelings and cross-reference the flower indications in chapter 2.

For chronic emotional states that call for multilayered treatment, place four drops of a combination flower remedy directly from the dosage bottle onto your tongue or, alternately, put four drops in a glass of water and sip. Repeat four times a day, over the course of three to four weeks. You'll know that your remedy is working as your challenges gradually become softened and the next layer is revealed. After a few weeks, you may forget to take your remedy, which is a sign that you no longer need that combination. This could happen before your bottle is empty. Then, repeat the self-reflective process and create a new combination remedy or choose a single flower to work with over the next few weeks.

Upon reevaluation you might notice that a particular challenge is only partially resolved, so the correlating flower (or flowers) would then need to be included in the new combination remedy. I rarely include the same flower for more than two mixtures in a row, yet sometimes I find it necessary to repeat a supportive flower in a future formula. This speaks to the fact that certain challenges are part of our behavioral makeup. What I find is that if certain flowers do need to be repeated, the resolution is quicker and acts more deeply each time. As you become more able to recognize your emotional habits and patterns, you more easily attune to the resonant energy, and transformation comes at a more rapid pace.

Why a Remedy Doesn't Work

The art of flower therapy is a beautiful dance with our internal experience. When the selected remedies are working in harmony with our inner balance, we can feel the flow. Troubles that plagued us become unimportant, our confidence rises, and fears dissipate. Yet, sometimes the balance is off, and we may notice that a remedy isn't offering as much support as needed. There are a few possible reasons for this.

The chosen flower isn't the right one: Sometimes we don't get to the deeper layer that needs to be addressed, and we choose a remedy on the basis of a superficial complaint. For example,

Jamie is concerned about difficulty falling asleep at night. He can't stop thinking about his many responsibilities, and he's worried that he won't be able to fulfill them. I offer him white chestnut, on the basis of his overthinking, and this helps only somewhat. When Jamie returns three weeks later, his mind is a bit calmer, but he still has anxious thoughts over his many responsibilities. The remedy that addresses this more fully is elm, since Jamie is feeling overwhelmed and benefits from the transformative medicine of organization and confidence in handling the tasks at hand.

The remedy isn't being taken at least four times a day: As with all practices and medicines, consistency is key. Dosage is important with flower therapy so that you receive the required amount to produce a shift. Also, creating time to take your remedy is a self-nourishing practice. You can enhance the experience by taking a few moments in a peaceful setting, perhaps outdoors, and recite a short mantra or affirmation.

There is an emotional block creating resistance to the healing process: This is a big one, and I've seen it a few times over the years. Psycho-spiritual practices and energy medicines allow for great shifts in awareness, but sometimes we are unprepared to open to the energetic shift. When someone takes a combination formula for several weeks and returns and still feels stuck, they may be immobilized in a state of trauma. In this instance, I use the single remedy of holly or wild oat for a couple of weeks, to clear the energy field. Dr. Bach believed that a disconnection from humanity and confusion about one's calling were two major detriments to well-being. Holly addresses the elements of hatred and jealousy that keep a heart closed, and wild oat addresses the elements of uncertainty around a vocational path. Holly is used for a more extroverted type, whereas wild oat is used for a more introverted type. Whenever one is addressing trauma or deeper psychological issues, the support of an empathetic psychotherapist is important and a wonderful pairing with flower therapy.

Flower Remedies and Affirmations

When I design healing programs for others, I recommend using the positive affirmations I created that correspond to each flower selected (available in my oracle deck *Listening to Flowers*). Although this practice is not part of Dr. Bach's original method, I find it aligns with his system quite nicely. By utilizing the resonant energy available through the spoken word, you begin to shift your perspectives and view challenges in a positive light, rather than focusing on the negative impacts of your symptoms. More than merely the "power of positive thinking," but the actual energetic response felt inside as you deeply engage with statements and goals that focus on transforming negativity and illness into positivity and healing.

The instructions are simple: Recite the affirmations that correlate with your current flower remedy, out loud, daily. Do this with the intention of evoking the healing energy of the flowers. Use the ones that most resonate with you day to day, focusing on only one or two each time. You can write them on a piece of paper and then tape it to your mirror to recite in the reflection each morning. When the words are difficult to speak aloud, this is instructional as to what holds you back from shifting your perspectives. In this way, it's possible to transcend and *include* all aspects of your experience to reach a state of greater wholeness.

CHAPTER 2

The Original

THIRTY-EIGHT BACH FLOWERS

There are thirty-eight flower remedies in the Bach system, and one combination formula. This section of the book divides the remedies into the seven categories of emotional challenges recognized by Dr. Bach in 1933 in *The Twelve Healers and Other Remedies*. The flowers are listed in his original order, with no known reason as to why he chose this sequence. I contacted several experts on this, including the Bach Centre in the UK, and his reasons remain an alchemical mystery.

When reading the flower indications, keep your notebook handy and jot down any flowers that feel relevant to you. Then refine your selection down to the most-fitting two to seven flowers. I've included journal prompts for each category, to help you delve more deeply into your emotional experience. It helps to close your eyes or look downward when you reflect on the questions.

FEAR

Rock Rose, Mimulus, Cherry Plum,
Aspen, Red Chestnut

Each time I reflect on the Fear remedies, I recognize how prevalent the challenge of fear is for humankind. I also wonder about Dr. Bach placing this category first in the system. It seems a primordial collective energy that can be seen as the basis for most suffering. It's interesting to think that fear has different ways in which it resides in the human soul. When we think of fear, we tend to think of simply being afraid of something: the dark, spiders, public speaking, or anything that can be named (mimulus). But there are other ways in which fear shows up in your daily life. Fear and worry for loved ones (red chestnut); an ominous sense of fear with a foreboding quality, for no known reason (aspen); fear that shows up in the form of terror or panic (rock rose). Then there's fear that leaves you feeling anguished with a loss of control (cherry plum). To be able to mindfully reflect on what type of fear you are experiencing helps you become empowered, courageous, and fearless in the face of such adversity.

Journal Prompts for Exploring Fear

What am I afraid of?
What do I notice in my body when I'm scared?
What is fear trying to tell me?

Rock Rose

Helianthemum nummularium

I am blessed with abiding calm and true peace.

Challenges: extreme fear, terror, nightmares
Transformations: calm, peace, security

The glowing light of rock rose amid dusty landscapes is indicative of the healing energy this flower emits. It clings to rocks, creating a golden profusion in gardens, parks, trails, and roadsides, and its medicine is displayed in this interplay of illumination and darkness. Thriving only in dry soil, rock rose's radiant glow displays the life force that revives a depleted terrain.

The keynotes of the rock rose condition are extreme fear and terror, which can be either acute or chronic. I use this flower mostly as part of the Rescue Remedy® formula, and if I do offer it singularly, it usually needs to be taken for only a few days to assuage the effects of frightful terror.

The Latin name "Helianthemum" refers to the solar force; so naturally, the transformative qualities of this golden flower are that of light. It is exactly this luminous energy that relieves the cold dread of fear, by bringing the essence of warmth to the body, and reenergizes life. The result is a calm, peaceful demeanor, connected to the support of a grounded physical presence. Inner strength is activated, and a sense of courage restored.

Rock rose is one of the five flowers in Rescue Remedy®, and its place in this combination bouquet is that of nerve stabilizer. We see the symptoms as terror in its most extreme form. The child who wakes from sleep terrified and screaming needs this flower. Eyes wide open, mouth agape, body rigid—all physical indicators of this emotional state. When my daughter was small, she went through a challenging growth process of experiencing regular nightmares about her loved ones dying. She would wake in the middle of the night, certain that something terrible would happen to the family. Rescue Remedy® helped her get back to sleep, but it wasn't until I started giving her rock rose throughout the day that the pattern shifted. At first, the nightmares became less, about every three nights or so, and after three weeks of taking the remedy they quieted altogether. Through the years, I've witnessed the transformation of many children and adults from terrified to tranquil, in rock rose's healing light.

Mimulus guttatus

I stand tall and know I am safe.

Challenges: fears that can be named, nervousness, timidity
Transformations: courage, safety, excitement

Of the five Fear remedies, mimulus is the most widely embraced, since each of us, at one time or another, has experienced fear related to something (or many things) we can name. "*What are you afraid of?*" is the question at the core of this remedy. When we can recognize a specific fear, we attune to the energy of the mimulus challenge.

As Dr. Bach described the mimulus type, "Fear of worldly things, illness, pain, accidents, poverty, the dark, of being alone, of misfortune. The fears of everyday life." Anything we can point to that scares us. It's a small feeling, where weakness and timidity are displayed. We may be quiet, afraid to speak out or stand up for ourselves.

A powerful contrast I notice with the mimulus transformation is that of increased excitement, or eagerness, for what was previously feared. There's a sense of bravery guiding us along with curiosity, rather than a feeling of fear holding us back with fright. Instead of trepidation, we welcome our experiences with courage and wonder.

A colleague of mine, Michelle, was going through a divorce, and she was struggling with her fears about being single again. She had grieved the loss of the marriage yet was at a stage where she felt unable to embrace her new independence. Michelle recognized that she was faced with fear about living alone, starting a new job, and the possibility of dating. Just thinking about these things would leave her feeling nervous and scared. As she confided in me, I suggested she try single remedy of mimulus for a few weeks. When we met for tea a couple of weeks later, Michelle's energy was upbeat, and she was smiling. She talked about buying some new furniture for her home, making friends at her job, and starting to think that it would be nice to go out on a date with someone she liked. As she talked, her eyes sparkled, and I commented that she seemed excited by all the possibilities. She paused, then reflected, "I guess I am excited! For the first time since the divorce, I can honestly say I'm looking forward to life, and I don't feel afraid of everything."

Cherry Plum

Prunus cerasifera

I find the stability to command my actions.

Challenges: fear of losing control, irrational
thoughts, impulsiveness
Transformations: self-possession, serenity, composure

Cherry plum remedy is not made from a cherry tree, but from a
plum tree with a cherry-sized fruit. An early sign of spring, the
flowers come alive in a profusion of white blossoms, full of the
promise of new life. This flower holds a special place in the Bach
system as one of the two Fear remedies (rock rose is the other) in
Rescue Remedy®. Cherry plum is a powerful flower, related to an
intense condition, and its medicine brings us back to a state of
rationality amid mental chaos—when we feel we are on the brink
of losing our minds.

An extreme fear of lacking self-restraint, the cherry plum challenge can often be seen as displayed in panic attacks, or any impulsive habits that are beyond our control. When we feel utterly outside our power, with an irrational fear of not being able to command our actions, and an inability to maintain composure, we fear we could be led down a path of doing harm to ourselves, or to others. Those who experience the cherry plum negative state chronically will benefit from focused care with a trusted therapist, alongside flower therapy.

The transformation is that of a self-possessed way of being. We become in command of our actions, rather than being swept up in our anxious *reactions*. Confidence is displayed in a steady, calm demeanor as we learn to trust in our serene mind to guide us. In extreme cases, cherry plum remedy can be used as often as needed, until a sense of composure is restored.

During the intensity of the pandemic, Andrea became plagued with extreme fear when going to the grocery store. She was able to get in her car and drive there, but when she arrived, she became filled with a feeling of panic. She sat in her car, gripping the steering wheel, anxious with fear of not being able to keep her cool while inside. All she could do was turn around and drive back home. In the days that followed, the mere thought of going to the store was enough to make her sweat with fear. I suggested that she use cherry plum acutely—two drops, four times a day—until the feelings of panic subsided. On the third day she was able to drive to the store. When she arrived, she felt a bit nervous, but she also noticed a sense of relaxation in her body, and a newfound peacefulness of mind that she didn't have before. Andrea was able to connect with her breath as she calmly entered the store and did her shopping. She continued the remedy for another two days, after which the fear completely subsided.

Aspen

Populus tremula

I embody unwavering courage.

Challenges: fear without reason, uneasiness, apprehension
Transformations: courage, steadiness, inner strength

Tall and trembling, rustled by the slightest disturbance, the shivering leaves of the aspen tree display the fearful energy present within this flower's challenge. Fear for no known reason is the keynote—when we feel scared and shaky on the inside, yet we don't know why. It's not the typical fear state, when we can name what we're afraid of, but more of a felt sense of fear that's dark and ominous.

The challenge can arise suddenly, without warning, day or night. Fear creeps up, with a sensation of shakiness at the core. A foreboding quality with a cold chill on the inside creates a subtle tremor within. There's a creepy, "haunted" feeling, as if something bad is going to happen, but we know not what, similar to when we awaken in fear from a nightmare and feel vaguely "spooked."

The remedy provides a sense of safety within. As courage is restored, our physical presence becomes steady and stable. We feel peaceful and calm on the inside as our nerves become stronger, and the trembling subsides. Inner strength arises from trusting that we are safe and secure. Paranoia falls away, and the previously sensed uneasy energy no longer casts an eerie pall.

In the first stage of the COVID-19 pandemic, when we all were quarantined to our homes, there was a scary, ominous feeling in the air—a fear that was unknown. Many of us were afraid of the virus, and of getting sick, but on a deeper level I witnessed a sense of vague apprehension that couldn't quite be named. Everything just felt weird and "off." As I met with clients, students, and friends, I began to hear a collective voice that resounded this energy of an unspecified uneasiness inside. Fear that produced a sense of shaking at the core of our beings, like nothing we've ever experienced before. I used, and suggested, aspen remedy to countless people, and as I witnessed the flower do its work, I noticed a sense of safety pervade throughout my healing community. As we felt more peaceful within, we became better able to trust in our collective experience and to release fear of the unknown. In aspen's healing light, we were guided by a steady presence of spirit, inner strength, and unwavering courage.

Red Chestnut

Aesculus carnea

I trust in the welfare of my loved ones.

Challenges: fear and worry about loved ones
Transformations: trust, inner peace

Red chestnut is one of the three *Aesculus* remedies within the Bach system (chestnut bud and white chestnut are the others), and it holds a unique place in the Fear category, since the remedy assuages a particular worry about our loved ones. Like the other "chestnut" flowers, the challenge relates to mental activity, as is metaphorically demonstrated in this tall tree's upward-reaching habit.

The anxious parent who imagines the worst when their child is away from them, or the person who is certain their partner has been in an accident when they're five minutes late, is an example of how this habit of "concern" keeps us shackled in fear. Ultimately, we cast a dark cloud over our relationships, since our connections are rooted in fearfulness. This precludes us from enjoying the freedom within our partnerships, as we allow fear to manifest as unhealthful attachments to those we love.

The magical transformation I've witnessed through the light of red chestnut is that of relational healing. Recognized as a psychological phenomenon, when one person begins to change for the better, the relationship takes on its own healing dynamic and grows. When we're able to let go of our fears and doubts about the safety of others, we create a resonance that is founded in trust and inner peace. In this way, our connections with others have the space to become stronger, grow, and flourish.

Several years ago, I had a profound healing with a red chestnut tree. My college-age son had traveled to Europe, by himself, for the first time. The day he arrived there, I awoke, worried for his safety. My husband and I went hiking at Fort Ord National Monument in Monterey, California, and my head was heavy with worry as I descended the trail. I shuffled on, not paying much attention to the flowering plants along the path. As we came around a bend, I was met with a towering red chestnut tree in full bloom! Bees buzzed in chorus, amid heavenly smelling blossoms. As my fingers reached up to touch the petals, the indication for red chestnut remedy dawned on me. I stood under the canopy, closed my eyes, and stayed in this magnificent presence for some time. As I drank in the essence of comfort and fearlessness, I envisioned my son's well-being and released any worries. This was a deep experience of being able to physically connect with the healing energy of the red chestnut flowers and embrace the medicine available within the felt vibration.

UNCERTAINTY

Cerato, Scleranthus, Gentian, Gorse, Hornbeam, Wild Oat

When you're able to view life through a positive lens, you can tap into a sense of conviction and assurance, which carries you forward. Yet, when the lens of negativity colors life, you can get stuck in a sense of uncertainty, which makes it difficult to achieve success. One typical challenge to feeling certain is seen as indecision, with an inability to make choices, whether about small details or major life events (scleranthus). Yet, there are several ways in which you might feel uncertain that go beyond decision-making. This might surface subtly as a lack of trust in your inner knowing (cerato), or perhaps more commonly in negativity about life, in the form of discouragement (gentian), and deeper still into hopelessness and despair (gorse). There is even a particular form of uncertainty that shows up as confusion about one's path in life (wild oat). Or, in the common state of procrastination, as you are unsure of how to activate motivation (hornbeam). The flowers in this category transform the negativity of doubt by providing you with the faith to follow the path before you, and a certainty to carry you through the many twists and turns of life.

Journal Prompts for Exploring Uncertainty

When do I feel confused?
What am I unsure of?
What do I know to be true?

Cerato

Ceratostigma willmottiana

I embrace my truths as pure knowing.

Challenges: inability to trust inner knowing,
seeking answers from outside sources
Transformations: enhanced intuition,
inner knowing, trust in self

Ethereal blue-violet blossoms of cerato flower are a captivating hue. This color is indicative of the third-eye chakra, our internal energy center that governs our capacity for intuition. The flower remedy is used to address a lack of trust in our intuitive faculties—when we constantly seek answers outside ourselves. In modern language, we use the word "google" as a verb. To "google" something means to use the internet to find answers to questions. We do this all too often and bypass the opportunities to reflect inwardly, to discover what we know beyond intellect. Although there's nothing wrong with seeking information, the challenge arises when we stop asking ourselves the questions first.

Cerato imbalance shows up as a feeling of not knowing. An uncertainty at the core that lacks faith in our process of discovery and abandons trust in our inner capacities. We continually give away our power as we seek answers from outside sources. We ask others for their input and often mislead ourselves by following someone else's path.

When we embrace the healing energy of cerato, we become true to an authentic way of being, grounded in self-wisdom. Our intuitive senses come back into balance, and we trust that we already have the answers within. Our truths are enlivened through a deep dialogue with our inner voice. That's not to say that we won't ever need the advice of trusted friends or experts, but knowing when it's time to turn to others is part of a balanced intuitive process.

"What do I know to be true?" This is one of my favorite questions to use as a self-inquiry practice with students. Let's try a little experiment now: With your eyes open, look upward, ask yourself the question, and note the first answer that comes. Now ask the same question, with your eyes closed, looking downward, and note the first answer that comes. Is there a difference? Usually, a downward gaze allows us to go inward with more ease and scan our interior landscape for nascent truths. When we ask ourselves, "What do I know to be true?," we exercise our innate powers of perception. In this way, cerato is a foundational remedy, and the one I use first when I lead trauma-healing workshops. Since abuse survivors often question their inner knowing, I guide students in using this flower as an opening remedy, so they can go deeper in their healing work and trust in what they "know to be true" at the core layer of being.

Scleranthus

Scleranthus annuus

I possess clarity as my decisions flow with ease.

Challenges: indecisive, difficulty choosing
between two things, wavering
Transformations: decisive, resolute, balanced

Scleranthus is an unusual, endangered plant, considered a
common self-sowing weed that grows in various habitats over
three continents. I've tried to grow it in my garden and failed.
You see, I couldn't understand what it wanted. Either there
was too much sun or too little, too much water or not enough—
everything I tried was not quite right. And such is the way of the
scleranthus challenge.

Like a pendulum that swings back and forth, the mind of the
scleranthus type is in constant motion. "Should I, or shouldn't I?"
"This one, or that one?" Those caught in this sway are in a perpetual

state of uncertainty, unable to choose between two things. This dilemma can be seen in major life transitions ("Which job offer should I take?"), as well as in minor, daily decisions ("Which shirt should I wear today?"). Whether the decision is great or small, the suffering is the same—a quiet, inward wavering.

Since there is much movement within the scleranthus challenge, when the remedy catalyzes a sense of equilibrium, there is a feeling of stillness at the core. Newfound trust in our decisions leads to a strengthened confidence. This provides the stability needed to achieve a greater mind-body balance. In this way, we can support our physical presence from the foundation of a steady, decisive mind.

Years ago, when I was suffering with digestive issues, one of the symptoms I experienced was intermittent dizziness. It would catch me off guard, and it was a little scary, as well as being uncomfortable and annoying. When I began to treat the symptoms on the basis of the emotions that were coming up, I noticed that the dizzy spells came on when I had to decide what foods to eat. The cleansing diet I was following was restrictive, and when it was time to go food shopping or cook meals, I felt confused. I typically don't question my choices, and this felt strange and unusual. I recall standing in the market, holding two different jars of bone broth and not being able to make a choice as to which one was better. The same thing would happen when I was at home, deciding what to eat. I would stand with the refrigerator door open, my eyes darting back and forth between the lentil stew and the split pea soup. My head felt like it was spinning, and I had to go sit down. All signs pointed to scleranthus, and since this was an acute challenge for me, using the remedy for just under a week was enough to assuage the dizziness. A rebalancing occurred that brought me back to my natural state of equilibrium, as I felt a renewed clarity of mind.

Gentian

Gentiana amarella

I have faith in the process of absolute success.

Challenges: discouragement after a setback,
disappointment, lack of faith
Transformations: conviction, acceptance, faith

It's a sinking feeling in the pit of my stomach when I know I've
made a mistake. This comes after I was progressing in my work,
and a tiny slip-up, or perhaps a grand error, created a mishap. I
get sullen, resigned to failure, until I recognize this as a gentian
state, and I resolve to get my mojo back and succeed. This is a
familiar plight for many of us; even those who typically triumph
can get caught in this vicious cycle of self-doubt, when things
don't go as planned.

The challenge appears seemingly out of nowhere, when we're
moving along, then a setback occurs, and we're left disheartened.

It could be a small oversight that goes unnoticed by others, or a big blunder that needs to be fixed; either way, it haunts our soul with disappointment. Discouragement is the keynote, since we can't seem to find our way back to faith, and negativity prevails.

Gentian's healing light offers us a renewed trust in the universe. We become certain of the process, failures and all, and find openness for what the deeper message might be. Gentian provides the conviction needed to embrace the best outcome, which draws us forward in overcoming our challenges with competence and ease.

Cindy came to see me to help with the challenges she was having around her waning fertility. Since she had just turned forty, and her daughter was almost seven, Cindy felt like this was her last chance to have another child. She had struggled with irregular menstrual cycles for most of her life and had difficulty conceiving. When we met, Cindy was forlorn at the prospect of not being able to get pregnant again. At this point, she rarely had a cycle, and she was doubtful that it would ever return. I suggested gentian and explained to her the indications. Right away, Cindy appreciated the recognition of her discouragement and understood how a renewal of confidence would give her the inner strength needed to heal. When we met four weeks later, she reported that her menstrual cycle returned briefly for a couple of days, which was more than she had in years. She felt hopeful and encouraged. We worked together for several months, and as Cindy went deeper into her healing process, her cycle returned more fully. We both were certain that her restored faith gave her a new outlook on life, with broader perspectives for her challenges. Cindy's focus shifted from discouragement for not being able to conceive, to conviction for taking optimal care of her body to support the best outcome.

Gorse

Ulex europoeus

Hope is illuminated in my soul.

Challenges: hopelessness, doubt, negativity
Transformations: hope, optimism, positivity

Gorse flower emits an expansive luminosity that produces a golden glow as far as the eye can see. A dense shrub native to the UK, it is indeed a sight to behold at the end of a long, dark winter. A thorny plant with an unlovely flower, yet bold in its assertion of life. Prolific and resilient, this, the vital essence that is portrayed in the healing power of gorse remedy.

Hopelessness is the keynote of this flower. In illness, the gorse challenge shows up as uncertainty of ever being healthy again. There's negativity hanging overhead, like a dark cloud. Interestingly, at the encouragement of others we will continue to try new methods for healing, even though we're sure that nothing will help.

This speaks to the fact that a ray of hope is indeed present, amid the doubt. In hopeless despair, we will struggle on, and this eventually leads to a transformation. Right at the edge of darkness, there emerges an inner light, and a restoration of the will to recover. Through this positive force, we find the strength to carry on and find renewal within.

Although it's not my place to treat others with a diagnosis of clinical depression, if there is one flower that I've seen lift others out of a "depressive" state, it's gorse. Frank was a young man who lived at home with his parents while they were going through a divorce. The family demise was incredibly painful. He was depressed and didn't think anything could help him. After several sessions together, Frank became more aware of how his relationship with his father had an impact on him. He recognized that the heavy energy his dad carried affected him deeply. He realized that he felt a sense of negativity for most of his life, which kept him stuck in doubt and darkness. With the aid of gorse, Frank could see the light at the end of the tunnel, and he felt more positive about his future possibilities. He immersed himself in work, which gave him relief from his family challenges, and he sought out a therapist to help him make sense of his childhood trauma.

Hornbeam

Carpinus betulus

My energy is renewed as I find motivation within.

Challenges: mental exhaustion, procrastination, lack of focus
Transformations: inspiration, motivation, clarity

It's that Monday morning feeling. When the mere thought of getting out of bed seems a chore. Motivation is lost, as a sense of procrastination prevails. Not wanting to take on the day, we feel indifferent to what lies ahead. Exhaustion of a weary mind, with a fogginess that lacks clarity, is the keynote of the hornbeam challenge.

This state is one I've seen often in adolescence and in anyone who's not feeling mentally stimulated. Perhaps the same old routine day after day has dug a rut in the road of life, or maybe there's simply not anything to look forward to. Whatever the case, there's just no inspiration.

This is usually an acute state that can be transformed quickly. Anywhere from one day to one month, the energy can be felt shifting to that of excitement and motivation. Inspirations arise as we become reenergized to engage with our work and hobbies, in ways that are novel and fresh. Although we may still dislike going to school or work, we undertake our day with more vitality and find joy within the routine. This can indeed lead us in the direction of new opportunities, as our visions come back into focus.

Throughout the pandemic I met with many people who had gotten COVID, myself and my family included. Brain fog was one of the symptoms that lingered for most people. I recall what felt like a mental hangover. There was a sense of fatigue that was in my head, after my body had recovered. I wanted to go back to work, yet I couldn't find the motivation. After about five days of using hornbeam remedy, I felt a definite shift one morning. I awoke with a sense of passion and inspiration that had been previously sapped. Hornbeam brought the healing process full circle, as my mind became reengaged and alert to possibilities. As the fog lifted, I felt more awake and less tired, and I could truly embrace my renewed state of mental clarity.

Wild Oat

Bromus ramosus

I follow my path and trust in my higher purpose.

Challenges: lack of direction, confusion about life path
Transformations: purpose, calling

Wild oat holds an important place in the Bach system, since the challenge relates to uncertainty of one's calling. Dr. Bach felt strongly about such a lack being a root cause of illness and strife. He was a firm believer that we all come into this world to manifest our own special gifts, which fulfill our soul journey—*"Every single person has a life to live, a work to do, a glorious personality, a wonderful individuality."* In this light he saw an utter soul demise when not being able to live out our vocational destiny. Wild oat is one of the two remedies (holly is the other) used to unblock "difficult" emotional states (see "Why a Remedy Doesn't Work" in chapter 1).

When we're plagued with confusion about our career path, we exhibit the typical wild oat challenge. We may be good at many things yet unable to choose one to aspire to, above all else. Perhaps there's indecision about which path to follow in school, or uncertainty about what we truly wish to share with the world. There's often a sense of having missed out, or not even knowing what our talents are. We passively question ourselves and bypass the opportunities to grow our skills. There's an emptiness felt inside.

The remedy can be taken alone for a few weeks to address this sense of void. What happens is that a layer of awareness emerges, and we become sure of our unique gifts as we uncover a newfound ability to refine them. We begin to follow our passion and claim our true calling, with certainty and fervor.

Sometimes wild oat healing begins as dissatisfaction with the work we're currently doing. Penny and I worked together for several months to address her severe physiological stress—extreme chronic fatigue, menstrual irregularities, digestive disturbances, and constant muscle pain. She commuted to New York City every day, by train, to work as the assistant to a high-powered celebrity hairstylist. Her job was glamorous and exciting but left her stressed and drained at the end of the day. As we went deeper into her healing program, Penny realized that she wasn't passionate about her job, but she wasn't sure what she would rather be doing. After using wild oat for a few weeks, she came to realize that she longed to follow her creative impulses in the field of acting. One day, Penny had enough and quit her job to follow her artistic path. Within a short time, she found success with writing, directing, and acting in several films, and she collaborated with numerous artists on various creative projects. As Penny became immersed in doing what she loved, her body grew stronger, and her symptoms cleared up.

NOT SUFFICIENT INTEREST in PRESENT CIRCUMSTANCES

*Clematis, Honeysuckle, Wild Rose, Olive,
White Chestnut, Mustard, Chestnut Bud*

Although the title of this category may sound unusual at first, as you reflect more deeply on the words you can understand the various ways in which this state of emotional challenge shows up in daily life. Attention deficiencies are acknowledged as a widespread cultural ailment (chestnut bud), repetitive thinking affects millions of people worldwide (white chestnut), and depression is at an all-time high (mustard and wild rose). There are even more-common, insidious ways in which lack of interest in the present moment shows up. When you catch yourself daydreaming and not hearing a word that was just spoken to you (clematis); when you're not able to feel joy in the present because of a longing for the past (honeysuckle); when your thoughts are stuck in mental chatter and you can't stop the noise in your head (white chestnut); when you are too exhausted to think at all and feel depleted (olive). The emotions are varied, but the element of disengagement is a key in recognizing this state of disinterest. When I sit with someone and there is disassociation, overthinking, exhaustion, or preoccupation with the past, I look toward the seven flowers in this category to imbue a sense of connection to the here and now.

Journal Prompts for Exploring Insufficient Interest

What do I notice about my mental activity?
What patterns do I see in my behaviors?
When do I feel the most engaged with life?

Clematis vitalba

I am clear and focused in this perfect moment.

Challenges: inability to focus, dreamy, clumsy
Transformations: focused, grounded, present

A prolific vine that spreads over fences and up tree trunks, clematis flower, when done blooming, produces a billowy, white head that floats off on the breeze, traveling far and wide—the perfect metaphor for the challenge indicative of the need for this remedy. Living in a state of fantasy, our thoughts drifting away, pulling us into dreams of the future.

When we're caught in the web of the clematis imbalance, we're disassociated from our bodies and can't focus on our current experiences. As a result, we may be accident prone and bump into things without realizing it. This is a familiar pattern for trauma survivors, and we may have learned to disconnect from our bodies early on as a coping mechanism. Often lost in daydreams, there's a surreal quality, since we don't feel fully awake or engaged.

An excellent remedy for when we find it hard to concentrate, clematis provides clarity and focus. One of the five flowers in Rescue Remedy®, clematis brings us back to the present moment. Rather than floating off into space, we reconnect with our bodies and become grounded here on Earth. As we release our habit of drifting into fantasy, we learn to use our imagination to bring alive our creative inspirations. In this way, we transform the challenge of preoccupation into empowered invention and artistry.

When Rachel came to see me, she had much self-awareness around her habit of daydreaming. As she went further on her healing journey, she realized a connection between her habit of dissociation and her early-childhood trauma. She remembered being small and "tuning out" whenever something threatening was happening. To comfort herself, she fantasized about all sorts of things. Now, as a grown woman, Rachel recognized how this habit showed up in her romantic relationships. As soon as she met someone, even if she wasn't particularly attracted to them, she concocted a whole fantasy in her head. She obsessed over every detail, imagining what it would be like if they were together. Clematis played a key role in Rachel's healing. After several weeks of using it, she noticed a steady shift in her mind. Rather than envisioning future, romantic scenarios, she felt a grounded presence in her body that kept her focused on what she experienced in the present moment. She became able to explore new relationships without spinning off into fantasy and could more fully enjoy the discovery of the here and now.

Honeysuckle

Lonicera caprifolium

I release the past and live for the sweetness of today.

Challenges: longing for the past, melancholy, homesickness
Transformations: contentment, joy, gratitude

The haunting fragrance of honeysuckle hearkens us back to a time of long ago and far away. A cloying scent that lingers, as we float away to a world of bittersweet memories. Clinging to garden fences, unwilling to let go, this sturdy vine beautifully illustrates the emotional challenge of bittersweet longing.

When I think of those who live in the past, wishing for happier times of youth, I reflect on this special kind of sorrow. There may be sighing, and talk of the way things used to be, or reminiscing of the "good old days." Every song on the radio that cries of lost love is a perfect example of this melancholic state. The parent who laments about the kids growing up, the aging person who tries to restore youthful beauty at all costs, the retiree who tells stories of their career heyday long after the fact—all would benefit from honeysuckle healing.

The transformation is a newfound sense of present-moment contentment. An ability to savor the sweetness of life today, in the here and now. A release of the past that allows for an integration of memories, and a comfort in knowing that in this moment, we are creating new ones. In this way, we embrace a sense of gratitude for all the joys that we have experienced.

As I write this, my youngest child will be reaching adulthood soon. Sometimes, I catch myself clinging to the past, with an aching nostalgia of when the kids were small. As I walk through the house, I longingly touch the kindergarten drawings that still adorn the walls. I realize this sense of sadness as a grieving for a time that I will never return to again. I'm pulled back even further to the 1970s, when I was a kid. In my mind's eye I can see the fireflies on a warm summer night, through the dusky backyard. I stay there awhile, and as my eyes become wet with tears, I recognize this desire for the past as a honeysuckle way. A few drops of the remedy, and my spirit is renewed. That's not to say that I won't get caught off guard again, perhaps by a family photo tucked into a corner or an old Mother's Day card at the back of the drawer, but each time I touch the sadness with honeysuckle's light, I more easily find peace in this present moment.

Wild Rose

Rosa canina

I engage with the beauty of life.

Challenges: apathy, disinterest in life, boredom
Transformations: vitality, enthusiasm, inspiration

Rose is arguably the most beloved flower of all time, the prominent subject of everything from poetry to perfumes, denoting love and captivation. With hundreds of varieties, this fragrant beauty has been cultivated throughout the world for centuries. The rose used in the Bach system is of the wild kind. Drought tolerant and incredibly fertile, the shrubs multiply throughout forests and gardens around the world and spread their intoxicating scent. Sharp thorns give contrast to such pure beauty and are indicative of the pain the wild rose type quietly suffers.

The wild rose challenge relates to the depressive state of apathy. There's a sense of sorrow and lack of luster in the way they look and the things they say—a heavy quality to their demeanor that is perceptible right away. When I meet with a client and they have a monotone voice, a sullen stare, and a sense of giving up on life, I turn toward the grace of this flower.

Just as a delicate rose has the power to invigorate the senses, this remedy activates a reconnection to life that's fresh and inspiring. In this renewal, we become enlivened, and we discover what truly excites us. Our passion is ignited, and we're reunited with all that is beautiful in the world around us.

Wild rose was a key remedy that led me on my path as a healer. Many years ago, I was at a crossroads in my career, and I became ill and disengaged from life. Not knowing where to turn, I shut down and literally couldn't do anything, save for simple daily tasks. I wasn't really living, but just barely surviving. In fact, I was so out of it that I wasn't even conscious of my experience at the time. One day, I stumbled upon a reading about wild rose. I connected with the description of boredom and disinterest, but, typical of the wild rose state, I didn't even want to try the remedy! A few days went by with me shuffling around thinking, "*What's the use?*" Then, as if a lightbulb went off, I realized that this passive attitude was exactly the indicator for needing the medicine of this flower. After using the remedy for several weeks, I became inspired to seek out the classes that led me to become a Bach flower practitioner.

Olive

Olea europoea

I am renewed with pristine vitality.

Challenges: exhaustion, depletion, difficulty
recovering from illness
Transformations: energy, renewal, strength

Ancient texts herald the many benefits of the olive tree, spiritually
as well as medicinally. A well-known symbol of peace, the met-
aphorical "olive branch" dates to biblical stories, and a wreath
of olive leaves was used in Greek mythology to denote victory.
For centuries, healers have used the leaf as an antiviral, and
people have used the fruit as a nutritive food source, with prolific
success. Clearly, the life force energy of olive abounds. This is
apparent in the way the flower remedy supports us in recovering
our strength after illness or physical exertion.

Exhaustion is the keynote when it comes to olive imbalance. This state is specific to having suffered with sickness, or anytime we've used our physical energy to the point of depletion. I've seen this remedy do wonders with the kind of exhaustion that follows the flu, as well as balancing the tiredness that comes with menstrual periods. Both the mind and body are spent, and there's a disconnected feeling that manifests as severe fatigue. We are so tired that we find it hard to care about anything.

Olive remedy imbues us with the inner strength necessary for full recovery. A vitality emerges that reenergizes us at the core. Deep within, there's a felt sense of renewal that makes it possible to get back into the groove of life. This was a key flower in helping clients and families recover from the aftereffects of COVID. Completely nourishing, olive feeds the body, mind, spirit, and soul in a primordial way.

A young mother I worked with years ago suffered from extreme exhaustion, several months postpartum. Camille saw me regularly throughout her pregnancy, as well as after the birth. At first, she had lots of energy, which surprised her, since she had heard how sleep deprivation affected new parents. She went back to work three months later and still nursed during the night. As the weeks went on, she became increasingly more tired, until eventually she was completely exhausted. Although she took good care of herself—slept as much as possible, exercised, and ate well—she couldn't seem to get her strength back. It was clear that her body had used up its reserves and needed to be replenished at the soul level. After a few weeks of using olive remedy, Camille's energy was restored and she felt a deeper sense of physical recovery. As olive provided energetic nutrients to her subtle body, her sleep became refreshing again, her spirit light, and her connection with life vital and nourishing.

White Chestnut

Aesculus hippocastanum

From stillness of mind, I embody calmness of spirit.

Challenges: overthinking, worry, rumination
Transformations: peace, calmness, tranquility

Tall and towering over neighborhoods, parks, and roadsides, the grand canopy of the white chestnut tree reaches up into the clouds. From the massive boughs, great, fragrant clusters form in early spring, their scent wafting through the air. Being in the presence of such grandeur indeed provides a sense of comfort and peace and seems a fitting sedative for the white chestnut state of an overactive, far-reaching mind.

Repetitive thoughts that cannot be stopped, constant worry with mental chatter, replaying the day's events—thinking about what we "should have said." Keeping us awake at night and overwrought during the day. We've all experienced these challenges, at one time or another, so much so that white chestnut is arguably the most widely used Bach remedy for the widespread "dis-ease" of overthinking.

The transformation is that of mental torture into mindful peace. A stillness can be felt at the center, and a conversion of unwanted thoughts into embodied presence. Our mind changes as we release clutter and embrace the spaciousness within. From this place of tranquility, we remain calm and find freedom from worry.

I've witnessed the healing energy of white chestnut with most everyone I've ever worked with or taught, since the need for peace of mind is great, and this flower is beautifully effective. A particular challenge I often hear reported by perimenopausal women is that of waking (perhaps several times a night) and not being able to quiet the mind. In the darkness, thoughts churning— trying to balance the checkbook, review the food-shopping list, or remember to call sis on her birthday. Many describe it as an internal alarm or bell that goes off. As our rhythms are derailed by physiological changes, our bodies may react with too much mental energy. In this way, white chestnut provides the psychospiritual shift needed to transmute the energy and quell our thoughts. I recommend keeping a bottle by the bed and using two drops when awakened by repetitive thoughts, as needed. Typically, shifts into peacefulness are reported with only a few doses. Naturally, if sleeplessness is a challenge that has plagued us for years, then the transformation to a calmer mind will take longer, with the likelihood of needing to address deeper emotional layers along the way.

Mustard

Sinapis arvensis

I awaken to my radiant bliss.

Challenges: sadness for no apparent reason, gloom
Transformations: joy, radiance, inner light

Living in Northern California, I'm lucky to experience blooming flowers year-round, and mustard always brings me joy as one of the earliest colors in late winter. As I drive past vineyards, my eyes fall on the golden glow that emanates between the rows. Radiant flashes of light amid a drizzly, gray landscape make my heart swell, and I forget any seasonal darkness. Each year, when I encounter this display, I reflect on how this light-filled energy emerges, seemingly at the perfect time, within the cycle of life.

The keynote of mustard is a sense of enshrouded gloom for no apparent reason—when there's a prevalent sadness that can't be attributed to any known cause. Such is the way of "seasonal affective disorder." Although we could say that the cause is lack of daylight, it's the *feeling* of sadness without knowing why that we are aware of when we're in this state.

The transformative energy of mustard is that of light-filled joy. An organic way of being that illuminates a sense of contentment, from a place of inner warmth. What may have felt daunting yesterday now has a brightness that can carry us forward into a new day.

Over the years, I've met with many first-time mothers. At some point, postpregnancy, it's not unusual for women to experience a depressive state. This is common, yet somewhat mysterious and misunderstood. Although there's a physiological shift, the bereft feelings occur on the subtle plane and are recognized as a void within. One woman I knew, Nina, described the energy this way: "It was as if I woke up under a rain cloud, but the rest of the world around me is in the sunshine. The baby is happy, my partner is happy, but I just feel heavy and dark, for no good reason." When I described to her the indications for mustard remedy, she instantly lit up and exclaimed, "Yes! This is exactly what I need!" The very idea of the flower's energetic properties sparked a renewed interest in her healing. By simply connecting with the effulgent medicine available from mustard, she was able to activate her process of positive emotional well-being, right away. After a few weeks of use, Nina felt a steady shift in her energy, and a newfound joy in motherhood. She recognized that she felt "more relaxed and happier around the baby, as if the clouds lifted and the warmth of the sun is in my heart."

Chestnut Bud

Aesculus hippocastanum

I cultivate wisdom as I learn from my mistakes.

Challenges: inability to learn from mistakes, repeating old patterns, difficulty retaining information
Transformations: wisdom, awareness, learning

Curiously, this remedy is not a flower, but the bud of the white chestnut bloom. The preemergence of the flower and all the information held within it—as a verb, to "bud" means to grow and develop. Within this framework, we can see how chestnut bud relates to shifting old patterns and transforming into a more evolved way of being.

The keynote of the chestnut bud challenge is an inability to learn from our mistakes, oftentimes repeating the same errors until the lesson is learned. We might recognize this state in minor ways, as we read the same sentence over and over, unable to comprehend the meaning, or in more-substantial ways, when we find ourselves replicating the same dysfunctional relationship, with different partners, again and again. No matter which, the result is the same—an inability to learn the lesson from our mistakes and bypass the opportunities for growth.

Chestnut bud remedy offers us the healing of present-minded awareness. As we become more focused and able to be fully available to our experiences, we gain deeper insight and greater wisdom. Whether through strengthening our powers of concentration or through receiving the lesson within the challenge, we become better able to accept the higher knowledge that's available to us.

Melody was an intelligent middle-aged woman who had just come out of a long-term relationship. When she contacted me, she was devastated by the breakup and was seeking ways to move through the stages of grief. As we worked together for over a year, Melody transitioned from distraught to reflective, as her awareness of the people she had past relationships with became clearer. We did various exercises over that time that helped her recognize the patterns she was repeating in her partnerships, and we chose to use chestnut bud to support her healing process. As she became more aware of making the same unhealthful choices in her relationships, she was able to change the course and do things differently. This led her to release what she recognized as old family patterns and embrace her divine wisdom of what a healthful relationship could be like. I witnessed the remedy open Melody to let go of old habits, which allowed for deeper relationships to form with new people.

LONELINESS

Water Violet, Impatiens, Heather

As I reflect on this category and those most in need of these flowers, I notice an underlying habit of self-isolation. There may be a tendency to spend time alone and not want to connect with others. The challenge lies in not feeling open enough to share, or receptive enough to receive. At times, you might become isolated to protect yourself from feeling exposed, or simply to keep to yourself if you are introverted by nature (water violet). Other times, you might notice a sense of anxious energy that keeps you moving quickly into the future, leaving others behind (impatiens). And then there might be a tendency toward self-obsession, which leaves you lonely as others are put off by this way of being (heather). This is an important category, in that healing work is catalyzed when you can joyfully be in the presence of others, with a calm demeanor and an open heart.

Journal Prompts for Exploring Loneliness

When do I feel most alone?
What happens in my body when I feel anxious?
What are some ways I can practice empathy for others?

Water Violet

Hottonia palustris

In reaching out, I cultivate inner warmth.

Challenges: aloof, introverted, isolated
Transformations: warm, connected, inclusive

Water violet is not a violet, as its name suggests, but a water primrose. The flowers poke out upright, above the water, while the rest of the plant happily resides hidden away, below the surface. Seems a befitting metaphor for the water violet type, who prefers to be left alone, out of view, to the potential challenge of isolation. One of the original "Twelve Healers," water violet personalities are typically quiet, and slow to intervene in the affairs of others. Often respected once acquainted, their leadership isn't usually obvious in the physical sense. Sensitive and deep, there's much good to say about this soulful way of being, until we end up alone.

The challenge lies in relying too much on ourselves, such that we no longer feel a need for the company of others. Perfectly content in our own private pursuits, we are our own best friend. Introverted by nature, the water violet type is self-reliant and prefers to do things solo. They are strong and on the outside often viewed as aloof or "snobbish"; problems arise through self-isolation. They find it hard to feel connected to others, and the sensitivity of this type could lead to a life of seclusion.

As we reflect on our loneliness, we may come to realize the importance of joining with trusted friends and loved ones, and the healthful benefits of being part of a community. Through water violet's medicine we open more, to create deeper connections, and we become better able to sustain our relationships through the balance of an inclusive heart. No longer feeling the need to lock ourselves away and retreat into privacy, we learn to lead with a warmth that allows for nourishing time spent alone, as well as time spent joining with others.

When we review the remedies in greater detail, we can each find one that is most relevant to our innate way of being. Water violet is mine. I completely relate to a deep need for privacy and prefer social gatherings with only one or a few people. I've been this way my whole life but became most aware of my habit of isolation after the birth of my daughter in 2005. We lived in a remote town on the Northern California coast, and it was unusual that five women who knew one another were pregnant at the same time. We all had older children and would sit in the bleachers at the Little League games and make small talk. I would sit quietly and keep mostly to myself. The months passed and we each had our baby, and some of the women were forming a mother's group to meet for walks. I found out through one of the women, whom I was close with, that I wasn't invited into the group. At first, I was hurt, but then quickly relieved. My friend was incensed: "How could they not invite you?!" When she confronted the others with this question, the answer was simple: "We didn't invite Dina because we knew she wouldn't come." This came as a lesson for me about how isolating myself deprived me of deeper community belonging. I didn't end up joining the mother's group, but I did find healthful connections in smaller groups, and I continue to nourish myself in this way that feels comfortable for me.

Impatiens

Impatiens glandulifera

I sail along effortlessly in the perfect stream of time.

Challenges: impatient, anxious, living in the future
Transformations: patient, calm, present

It's interesting to think that the challenge of impatience can lead us to a place of loneliness. When we look at the habit of the impatiens flower, we witness an explosion of seeds as the blossoms are lightly tapped with a finger. This speaks to the "explosive" nature and erratic motions of the impatiens type. It is within this activity of forward movement that we can find ourselves alone.

The challenge relates to a quickness of body and mind, which outpaces others. In this way, we prefer to work by ourselves, so as not to get slowed down. There's a physical sense of momentum that can be felt as anxiousness in the body, with a need to do. Those who benefit from this remedy are always ahead of the crowd, moving and thinking quickly, often finishing others' sentences. There's a great annoyance or anger inside when things are moving too slowly, as seen in the typical "road rage" scenario.

One of the flowers in Rescue Remedy® formula, impatiens imparts a sense of calmness at the core. Bringing us back to the present moment and slowing us down enough to integrate inner peace, which, in turn, supports our healing process. Patience and tolerance are felt, within an effortless flow of time. Rather than feeling anxious and sped up, our bodies feel relaxed enough to slow down.

Quite often in my work with others, I see impatiens as a common type remedy. Perhaps it's a sign of the times. Since the world is moving seemingly more quickly than ever, it makes sense that we would need an elixir of pause. I embrace impatiens as one of my personal flowers. Early on in my flower remedy studies, I could relate to the habit of moving too swiftly into the future, and how this would often leave me impatiently waiting. I had trouble sitting still for meditation and got irritated when others would take "too long." The remedy taught me how to savor the moments spent in wait. Although I'm prone to the habit of impatience, and it occasionally recurs, what I notice is that each time it arises, I gain more tolerance. Sometimes simply attuning to the vibration of the affirmation alone, I can feel my being grounding into the present moment. As I slow down and recite the words, I connect with the essence of patience as the flower remedy does its work on a subliminal level.

Heather

Calluna vulgaris

I join with others through selflessness.

Challenges: overtalkative, self-obsessed, clingy
Transformations: receptive, mindful, selfless

Of the three flowers displayed in the Loneliness category, heather is the type that most longs for connection with others. Dr. Bach referred to the challenge associated with heather as "buttonholing," meaning that it's difficult to escape their hold once they have your ear. In this way heathers end up lonely, since their clinginess is suffocating to all whom they connect with.

The irony of this challenge is that while trying to make friends, they inadvertently drive people away with too much talking about themselves. The elderly person who corners us in the market, asking question after question about what they should buy; the friend who relentlessly talks about their life, without pausing to hear about ours; the neighbor we barely know who stops us on the street to fill us in on what they've been up to for the past year. Self-obsession disguised in an overfriendly demeanor is the keynote of the heather imbalance. The sad part is that these types are painfully lonely at the core yet remain so by not being able to selflessly receive others.

The transformation comes about when we learn how to communicate properly, simply by listening. Being able to altruistically hold space for others allows for true friendships to form. By learning to trust that we don't have to push ourselves onto others, we create relationships built on mindfulness and care.

Heather is one of the hardest flowers to suggest to a client or student, in that it's tricky to relate the challenge without it sounding like an insult. "You talk about yourself too much" is a bitter pill to swallow for most. A few years ago, I taught a flower remedy class, and I would pair students together so they could practice prescribing for one another. After class one day, my student Bella contacted me and told me about her experience meeting with her classmate. She was certain that her partner needed heather, since they spent the entire session focused on her needs, such that Bella couldn't get a word in before the class time was up. I decided to reach out to the talkative student with compassion, since I recognized her loneliness. It turned out that she was a single mother without any family nearby, and she was starved for connection. I suggested she try heather remedy, to feel less anxious about her loneliness. She appreciated my empathy and used the remedy for several weeks. As she continued to participate in my classes, I was able to witness how much more reflective she became about her feelings, and how much more receptive she became in being there for others. It was a lovely transition into a more self-assured way of being.

OVERSENSITIVE to INFLUENCES and IDEAS
Agrimony, Centaury, Walnut, Holly

This category reflects feelings of vulnerability with a need to develop a stronger flow of boundaries. You can allow energy that feels supportive and nourishing to flow in at a healthful level, or you can develop the inner strength to keep energy out that feels unhealthful or burdensome. You may feel a need to protect yourself from any confrontation by hiding your true feelings (agrimony). Or perhaps, you become overly sensitive to the wants of others, at the expense of your own needs (centaury). Feelings of anger, hatred, or jealousy reflect harsh judgments that lead you to feel troubled by the behaviors of others (holly). More subtly, empaths, highly sensitive people, and anyone who *feels* external energy may need to create an energetic barrier to protect emotional well-being (walnut). The flowers in this category provide a sense of security, and an ability to be true to yourself.

Journal Prompts for Exploring Oversensitivity

What makes me feel vulnerable?
What am I angry about?
What are my needs?

Agrimony

Agrimonia eupatoria

I am confident to express my true feelings.

Challenges: hides true feelings behind a facade, inner turmoil
Transformations: emotional honesty, inner peace

Hard to discern, yet more common than we realize, the keynote of the agrimony challenge is hiding our troubles behind a carefree facade. We've all known someone, or have been that person, who puts on a happy face, although suffering on the inside. Sometimes it's minor, and we just don't want to burden friends or colleagues with our problems, so we smile and push through. But the agrimony state can also be a cover for deeper issues.

With a sense of inner turmoil, the agrimony way is to quietly suffer, alone. The detriment falls on us as we hold the pain in and don't express what we feel. Extremely uncomfortable with confrontation of any kind, we will literally grin and bear it, rather than let others know our torment. This comes at a steep cost of lacking emotional honesty with others, but, worst of all, with ourselves. When we're in this state, we run the risk of giving in to addictive behaviors, since we might use substances to mask the pain.

In agrimony's healing light, a confidence emerges. As we become able to connect with and accept our inner experience, we allow our true feelings to come forth. When we touch our emotional truths within, we develop authenticity that can be shared with others. Our armor falls away, giving rise to tranquility, which makes us feel safe in our self-expression.

When I first met with Denise, she was smiling and didn't have much to share. She wanted help in overcoming a phobia and had trouble opening up. Denise was a creative, intelligent woman, and she recognized how her habit of tamping down her feelings left her tense at the end of the day. There were many instances where she wanted to tell her boss about the issues she was having at work, but instead she held it in and suffered miserably. At the end of our first healing session, I told her the flowers I recommended, with agrimony at the top of the list. I explained to her the indications and how the remedy would help her be more open with others and express how she feels. She quietly listened, then asked, "What if I don't want anyone to know how I feel?" This question came as confirmation of her need for agrimony! That said, Denise did not want me to add it to her formula, and since I always honor that we are each our own best healer, I did not include it. Several months and many remedies later, Denise worked through the layers of emotional challenge that prepared her for agrimony. She went on to benefit from its healing essence, which led her to express her true feelings and find tranquility within. This is a beautiful illustration of the right flower *at the right time.*

Centaury

Centaurium umbellatum

I fulfill my own needs with a strong will.

Challenges: weak will, subservience, self-sacrifice
Transformations: divine will, independence, self-care

Centaury's tiny pink flowers spread wide on the perimeter of loamy hiking trails. What's striking to me about the blossoms, aside from the vibrant star-shaped petals, are the golden-yellow centers, which emit a luminous glow from the core. I'm reminded of how this relates to the third "chakra" energy center, at the solar plexus, between the heart and stomach. This area of the body is represented by the color yellow and is symbolic of the energy of divine will. It's no wonder then that centaury comes to the rescue for the challenge of self-sacrifice when we need to strengthen our powers of self-determination.

The overwrought housewife who takes care of everyone's needs to the detriment of her own; the overworked assistant who can't say no to more responsibility, to the impairment of his social life; the overextended therapist who spends all day compassionately listening to others, without making time to talk with trusted confidantes about her problems. The keynote of the centaury imbalance is a definitive lack of self-care; putting the needs of others first, to the point of not even recognizing what it is *we truly want* from life.

For many of us, the habit of catering to others is so deeply ingrained that we feel that being needed *is* our path. Since centaury's light shines from within, our sense of divine will becomes activated, such that we begin to reflect what it is that calls to us, to explore. A sense of honoring ourselves arises, and we understand our needs more clearly than we did before. Nourished from this source, we're propelled forward on our own path with determination—no longer depleted by overgiving, but energized by a balanced sense of self-giving, which creates a strong foundation from which to nurture others.

Iris had a habit of never turning down an opportunity to serve. She was a kind, compassionate person who wanted to do all she could to help relieve the suffering of others. When we met, she was running two businesses and volunteered with four organizations. Although busy, she noticed how empty she felt. Over many sessions, her discomfort with having all this responsibility became more obvious. She knew there was more for her in life, but she was too overextended to have any time or energy left to search for it. Centaury was called for, and over the course of two months Iris was able to let go of half her commitments and embrace the ones that truly fed her soul. As she focused her attention on less, she showed newfound inspiration and vigor.

Walnut

Juglans regia

My boundaries are resilient as I encounter external forces.

Challenges: difficulty adjusting to change,
vulnerable, easily swayed
Transformations: adaptable, protected, self-possessed

Walnut is well known for its dense, secure shell, which safeguards the fruit within. This boundary keeps away animals and environmental disturbances, so that the nut inside can continue to mature and reach fruition. It is this outer protection that exemplifies one of walnut flower's energetic attributes. Unusual within the Bach system, walnut has three distinct indications for use, which makes it stand out as a favorite among flower remedy enthusiasts. My Bach teacher Nancy uses it as a powerful purification tool to cleanse her space. When I asked Patricia Kaminski of the Flower Essence Society which is her most beloved of the

Bach flowers, her answer was walnut. The multifacets of the walnut challenge show up regularly when I hear stories from clients, students, and friends of feeling overly sensitive to energy, having trouble adapting to hormonal changes, or struggling with ending that stale relationship.

One of the powerful applications of walnut is for protection from outside influences, when we "feel" and absorb the energy of others, which may accumulate throughout the day and call for a psychic "detox." Walnut is a key remedy for therapists, counselors, empaths, and anyone who feels deeply affected by the energy fields of others. Another important use is for when we have difficulty adjusting to change. Moving, starting a new job, aging—anytime adaptation to new situations or experiences proves to be challenging. Then there's an even more subtle state that points to the need for walnut remedy: when there is an unwanted connection to a person or place, and a sense that the ties need to be severed. This is a threshold experience, where one foot is through the door yet there's an energetic bond holding us back from taking the final step.

Walnut supports these transitional times by creating an invisible boundary, which shields us from vulnerability and sensitivity felt when we're around others or amid too much stimulation. Walnut ushers us through change with ease, allowing for a smooth passage. And sometimes walnut can provide the last "push" that we need to release what no longer serves us. The varied ways in which walnut provides support are interwoven to create a stronger sense of self and enhanced resiliency.

I turn to this powerful flower ally regularly in my personal life as well as in my work with others. One such transformation I witnessed was a remarkable example of walnut remedy used to treat an animal. Laura contacted me to explore using flower remedies for her cat, Jasmine, who was mysteriously losing hair and acting fearful. She heard that animals are particularly receptive to energy medicine, and since she was having no luck otherwise, we decided to have a session together. Upon deeper reflection, Laura realized that Jasmine started losing her hair when her husband's daughter came to stay with them, which coincided with Laura traveling more often for business. It became clear that Jasmine was suffering from stress around the sudden changes in her environment, in addition to feeling vulnerable about having the new family member in her space. I suggested using walnut remedy to provide Jasmine with the protection she needed to feel safe, as well as the comfort she needed to adapt to the transitions in her environment. After about a week of use, the cat's demeanor gradually shifted, as she spent less time hiding and more time with the family. As she adjusted to the new conditions in her home, she became calmer and more relaxed, and her hair began to return.

Holly

Ilex aquifolium

My heart expands in universal love.

Challenges: jealousy, hatred, spite
Transformations: compassion, harmony, love

Red berries are part of the energy displayed in the holly plant, the color denoting intensity, anger, and blood. The serrated leaf embodies a sharpness that cuts, symbolic of rage, hatred, and suffering. Intense emotions at the core, holly holds a place of particular importance in the Bach system as the remedy that guides us toward our unique place within the human family, by opening our hearts to compassion. Dr. Bach placed much emphasis on the significance of participation in the collective humanitarian experience and keenly understood how a disconnection from such led to deep suffering. He saw a closed heart as a life void of love and joy.

In "The Twelve Healers," Dr. Bach describes the need for holly remedy as "for the different forms of vexation." Hatred, jealousy, spite, malice, rage, dissatisfaction, and agitation are the harsh taskmasters that halt us from experiencing loving connections with others, and within ourselves. Perhaps the worst part of these turbulent emotions is that we feel terrible on the inside. And at the deepest layer, there is ultimately an unmet need for love.

Holly energy heals us by creating a sense of safety and security within, which leads to an opening of the heart and a release of malice. We feel an expansion of our true selves as we feel compassion for and from others, in a way that supports belonging to a greater community. As our capacity for love is strengthened, we become more in tune with the heartbeat of life, and we find our own rhythm within the fold of humankind.

"A Christmas Carol" by Charles Dickens can be interpreted as one of the best illustrations of the holly challenge, as displayed in the character of Ebenezer Scrooge. A lonely, selfish miser, Scrooge shows disdain for his employees and neighbors and goes about his day grumbling and full of hatred. Caring only about money, he treats others unfairly, with disregard for their needs. As he is shown his past mistakes and future demise in a series of dreams or "visions," his heart is softened as he awakens to fearing a lonely death. We witness his transformation to that of a joyful, compassionate community member who leads with generosity and receives warmth and kindness in return. The story illustrates how a loving connection with others is a foundation for a long, happy life.

DESPONDENCY or DESPAIR

Larch, Pine, Elm, Sweet Chestnut, Star-of-Bethlehem,
Willow, Oak, Crab Apple

This is the category I turn to first to alleviate deep sorrow (sweet chestnut), trauma (star-of-Bethlehem), or any feelings that contribute to negative self-judgments (crab apple) and limiting beliefs (larch). When there is guilt and shame (pine), or blame (willow) present, I look toward these flower allies to act as a balm for the soul. These emotions are the harsh ones that inhibit you from feeling your inherent goodness and self-worth. Other ways that despondency or despair might show up are either in feeling overwhelmed by too many tasks (elm) or, conversely, in the habit of overdoing to the point of exhaustion (oak). The transformative effects of these remedies speak to a sense of peacefulness, nourishment, and self-love.

Journal Prompts for Exploring Despondency or Despair

What can I let go of?
How can I give myself more nourishment?
What brings me peace?

Larch

Larix decidua

I know that I am enough.

Challenges: lack of confidence, repressed self-expression
Transformations: confidence, creativity, self-assurance

The multifacets of the larch challenge are displayed in the insidious ways we doubt our capabilities and devalue our worth. How we question ourselves, and how we hold ourselves back, for fear of not being good enough. There is a deep feeling of lack at the soul level, which is different from being afraid. There's a void in our self-confidence; a mistrust in our ability to succeed, so we might not even try.

Larch is a much-needed remedy that relates to a universal challenge of low self-worth. We compare ourselves to others, certain that we are not quite good enough. In this way, we engage in self-sabotage, since we set ourselves up for failure by not believing that we have what it takes to succeed. An excellent remedy for artists, musicians, performers, public speakers—anyone who feels unable to freely share their talents and gifts.

In larch's healing light, we become able to express ourselves with inner strength and confidence. A self-assured way of being emerges, since we know that what we have to offer is powerful and wonderful, in its own unique way. We let fall away any comparisons and allow our work and creative endeavors to flourish with self-assurance.

Jade came to see me about her struggle with what she recognized as low self-confidence. She recently graduated college and felt unable to move forward in her chosen career. When we met, Jade worked at a café and secretly aspired to attend grad school. She felt passionate about this pursuit, yet she didn't want to apply, since she was sure she would fail. Jade recognized that she was holding herself back by not believing in her skills and talents. She also became aware that this same feeling restrained her from creative self-expression. We worked together for many months, and larch was instrumental in activating her confidence to assert her expressive personality and honor her abilities. From here she became able to assuredly follow her career path and develop her skills.

Pine

Pinus sylvestris

I am worthy and deserving of life's gifts.

Challenges: guilt, shame, self-judgment
Transformations: self-acceptance, worthiness, self-love

Pine is one of my very favorite flower remedies, since it is a much-needed elixir in a world full of guilt, shame, and self-blame. Most of us are healing from past trauma, and a vital step in the recovery process is learning how to forgive ourselves. A keynote of this flower is constantly apologizing for every little error, even if it wasn't our fault. Pine shows us how to enact self-forgiveness and liberates us from the negative perceptions that we cast upon ourselves.

The challenge often shows up in the form of self-judgment. Anytime we catch ourselves in disparaging self-talk, we meet our inner critic, ready to take us down if we let them. In our mind's voice, we hear loud and clear the derogatory words we wouldn't use on others. The guilt wells up and shame emerges, as we're left in a cacophony of despair.

The gentle shift of emotions can be seen as a renewed sense of self-esteem, self-love, and self-worth. As we release the negative mindset that binds us to our wounds, we emerge empowered, realize our true value, and find freedom within.

I discovered pine as a foundational remedy for healing the emotional consequences of trauma early on in my work with others. When I first began practicing as a health-and-wellness coach, I quickly became known as a sexual-abuse-recovery coach. I didn't advertise as such, and I didn't have a therapist's license. What I did have was a willingness to be present with others, listen attentively, and truly empathize with their stories. As I heard similar echoes of women's stories, day after day ("I'm so stupid," "Why did I let that happen to me?," "It's my fault"), I reflect on pine as an elixir of self-love for those who are bereft of self-compassion. Each time I hear such sentiments, I offer pine's healing energy and watch the conversation change to "I see that it's not my fault," "I deserve to live a life of happiness," "I love myself."

Ulmus procera

I trust that I will accomplish everything set before me with ease.

Challenges: overwhelm, stress, burden
Transformations: composure, organization, ease

As I reflect on the energy of the tree flowers, I recognize a particular sturdiness and strength provided from their solid, regenerative foundation. Through the years I've gotten to know elm remedy intimately, and I've learned to embrace the support offered whenever I feel overwhelmed by my many responsibilities. I'm a doer. This is usually a good thing, since I can be depended upon to successfully juggle, and complete, many tasks at once. But sometimes the balance tips, and a wary question arises: "Will I be able to handle it all?"

In elm's imbalanced state, there's a sinking feeling. An utter sense of inundation that feels heavy and burdensome. A sense of overwhelming stress that signals to our minds that we simply cannot handle the magnitude of our tasks. We worry and feel like we should just give up.

The remedy provides an uplifting essence that is felt as a confidence in our effortless capability. There's a shift as we begin to organize our time more efficiently and seek the systems we need to succeed. Doubt fades away as we find the composure needed to bring our work to fruition, with ease.

Stan was a successful university department head who suffered from distressing thoughts first thing in the morning. He would wake early, usually before the sun was up, and not be able to return to sleep. He lay there in bed, plagued by all the commitments he had taken on. He had more than a restless mind, and his body felt burdened as he mulled over his daily chore list. In our work together, he recognized that when he had too many responsibilities on his plate, he felt overwhelmed and couldn't rest until all was complete. Stan worked though the layers of healing that brought him to elm, which ultimately helped him to be better able to organize his time and resources in a way that made it easier to accomplish his workload. In this transformation, his body became more relaxed, he felt less worried, and his sleep improved. As he learned to balance his time and energy better, he no longer felt stressed about whether he was capable, and he began to trust that he indeed would be able to do all that he committed to do. With the aid of various subsequent flowers, he also learned how to set stronger boundaries, and not to say yes to everything asked of him. It was the foundation of elm that provided the fortitude to catalyze such a change.

Sweet Chestnut

Castanea sativa

As I travel through darkness, my spirit becomes light.

Challenges: anguish, darkness, despair
Transformations: serenity, lightness, peace

The sweet chestnut challenge is described as a dark night of the soul. I've come to recognize the related traits as deep sorrow right at the surface, where tears easily flow. A unique state of mourning with overwhelming sadness that's too much to contain and easily spills over.

A keynote is that of crying. When I witness those in a likely sweet chestnut state, the welling up of tears serves as confirmation. Beyond shock or initial sadness, it's a painful hopelessness that feels unbearable, yet somehow we persevere, seeking the ray of hope that carries us forward, but we can find no way out.

A deep remedy, sweet chestnut's light washes over us and renews our souls. Despair moves through us with more ease as we feel held in the peaceful glow, not turning away from the sorrow but leaning into the transformative quality of the darkness. To be able to go inward, touch deeply our anguish, and find acceptance is the path of healing.

Kate was the sister of a good friend who suddenly passed away at a young age. Our small community was devastated when we had lost this man. I reached out to Kate to offer her a flower therapy session, knowing that she was suffering deeply through this loss. When she came to see me, she looked soft and was quiet. We had briefly met a few times before, and I recalled her being much more talkative and vivacious. Now, her deep sorrow was apparent. I knew right away that she would benefit from sweet chestnut remedy, and as she opened she began to cry freely. We spent most of the time together in silence as the tears washed through her and released some of the pain that had been held inside. After a while we talked about what she was feeling, and she agreed to use sweet chestnut remedy to help her process the despair. When we met three weeks later, Kate was smiling, almost glowing. She talked about being incredibly sad for a week or more and just sitting and crying for hours on end, until she felt a sense of relief as a newfound energy pulsed through her. We talked about her transformation, and she described it as if the mourning had opened the door to explore a spiritual connection with her brother, which felt comforting. Kate was still sad about not being able to see or talk to her brother, but she felt more at peace with his departure and had the strength to move forward in the grieving process.

Star-of-Bethlehem

Ornithogalum umbetelatum

I know that I am greater than my sorrow.

Challenges: shock, trauma, grief
Transformations: comfort, healing, strength

A small, white, six-pointed star flower shoots out of the early springtime soil, heralding hope after the long, dark winter. Star-of-Bethlehem is prominent in Rescue Remedy® as the savior of Bach flowers. Almost miraculously, this remedy is known to address deep-seated trauma. Whether from abuse that was suffered years ago, or from the aftereffects of a recent accident, star-of-Bethlehem provides a strong foundation that makes it possible to transcend our deepest wounds.

There's a numbness that appears as a dazed expression, with a monotone voice. Like a soul that's frozen over in shock, unable to exhibit emotion. A deep grief that cannot be accessed, and star-of-Bethlehem's challenge is easy to discern yet difficult to touch, since we feel shackled by trauma.

Comforter of sorrows, the transformation comes when the remedy shines its light from within to soothe our trauma, and healing feels possible. What was previously stuck in despair can now move toward catharsis as our soul candle is lit and guides our path.

The stellar effects of star-of-Bethlehem are apparent in my work with trauma survivors. I've witnessed the healing energy comfort those in a state of shock after having experienced loss, be it a loved one, job, or home. One such powerful healing occurred when I worked with a ten-year-old girl after the loss of her parents. Lily was in foster care after the death of her father, and her mother was unable to care for the family. It was heartbreaking to see Lily walk into my office, face sullen, eyes round, staring blankly. She stood before me, small and meek, yet in a few words she was able to convey the pain she felt inside. I offered her star-of-Bethlehem as a first-course remedy and explained to her the indications and potential transformations, and she eagerly accepted. Lily liked the idea of having her own flower remedy in a bottle, and as she took the first dose before leaving, I could see a tiny smile faintly emerge. We met again three weeks later, and as soon as she walked through the door, I noticed a bounce in her step. She excitedly told me how she carried her remedy with her and took it regularly. After we talked further, it became clear to both of us that star-of-Bethlehem had unblocked the trauma and allowed Lily to feel the difficult emotions of grief. As her energy began to revive, she was better able to work with her therapist and move through the various stages of healing.

Willow

Salix vitellina

I release blame and embrace responsibility.

Challenges: resentment, bitterness, blame
Transformations: acceptance, responsibility, forgiveness

Indigenous people, herbalists, and wise women have been using willow bark for centuries for its medicinal benefits. Salicin, the chemical found in this plant, is the precursor to what we know of as aspirin. There's a notably bitter taste to this compound, and such is the keynote of the emotional challenge that is indicative of willow remedy. "It's not fair!" is a common cry from those in need of this flower. When I'm guiding someone and they're focused on how others are responsible for their suffering, I refer them to willow.

The challenge arises as resentments surface—feeling as if "they" did something to create your problems. Jumping from one blame to another, the willow type makes a solid argument as to why it's always someone else's fault. Perhaps the thing that is most destructive about this way of seeing the world is that it feels terrible on the inside and holds one back from the inner freedom necessary to progress in life. There's a tension from clinging tightly to condemnation that results in stunted relationships with others. Indeed, blame is a bitter pill to swallow.

Yet, sometimes the bitter can be healing, and willow acts as an emotional purging of all the acidic, sharp stings of life. The transformation that this flower offers is a sense of forgiveness for what we perceive as the wrongdoings of others. An acceptance of the fact that we're all human emerges, and a willingness to take responsibility for our own actions and mistakes comes to the fore. Such virtues, when well developed, contribute to a world of greater good.

Years ago, I worked with a woman, Rita, who was struggling with her longtime husband's advanced dementia. I clearly recall Rita's angst as she showed up with much sorrow and anger at her challenge of caregiving her husband through his illness. She came to see me because she recognized that the resentment she was carrying felt like she was "beating herself up on the inside." She felt indignant at how unfair her plight was. Although Rita's feelings were valid, the sense of being stuck in resentment was holding her back from developing the skills she needed to manage this difficult challenge. She felt tormented and betrayed by life. After using willow remedy for a couple of months, she emerged with a sense of softening of her harsh reality, which led her to the next layer of healing, which was grief. Willow had provided her with the opportunity to forgive her fate and take responsibility for finding ways to nourish herself through the process.

Oak

Quercus robur

I listen to my body and take time for replenishment.

Challenges: overworked, inability to rest, dutiful
Transformations: fortitude, resilience, renewal

Mighty oak, strong and sturdy, provides lavish amounts of food and shelter for wildlife as well as continually supplies humans with fresh air and shade. Truly a miraculous being, oak stands tall and proud. Until it falls heavily. This characteristic is displayed in the tragic disease known as "sudden oak death," which isn't really "sudden" but can take many months or years to take down the steadfast tree. This exhibit is quite telling of the oak challenge, since we will endure many burdens for long periods of time until we are forced to heed the message to set down our heavy load.

Overwork to the point of potential demise is the keynote of the oak type. Reliable, capable, and strong, this personality displays a slow, steady, methodical approach, which keeps them productive. The challenge arises when they don't know when to stop, until it's too late. We may fall ill or inadvertently hurt ourselves, such that our bodies are signaling for us to rest. Even then, the oak tendency is to push on and take care of the work that needs to be done, even in illness.

As oak's essence begins to bring us back into balance, we recognize the importance of consistent rest and replenishment within our cycles of work. In this way, we can continue to be effective through giving ourselves the support we need to maintain our workload. We carry on with a renewed sense of power, aligned with our innate abilities of resilience and strength.

Grace was a holistic physician who came to see me to address her feelings of "burnout" around her work. She enjoyed a lucrative private practice and was usually energized by her patients, until she recently noticed that her work felt like a duty. Grace exhibited the typical oak pattern—hardworking and quite capable, long days at the office, without much time for anything else—her workload far outweighed the time she spent to replenish herself. After a deep conversation, she realized that she wanted to release some of her commitments, and she agreed to use oak remedy over the following month for support. About three weeks later I got an email from Grace, telling me that she was still working too hard and that she wondered if the remedy was helping. When I asked her if she'd been taking it four times a day, she replied that she didn't have time. Typical of the oak type, keeping her head down in work, Grace didn't "have time" for self-care, and she never returned.

Crab Apple

Malus pumila

I welcome imperfection as opportunity for growth.

Challenges: negative self-image, lack of self-love,
fixation on flaws
Transformations: acceptance, self-love, cleansing

"This is the remedy of cleansing," Dr. Bach simply states of crab apple in his seminal work *The Twelve Healers and the Four Helpers.* Treating a flawed feeling at the core that prevents us from fully accepting ourselves as we are, crab apple is one of the most universally called-for flower remedies for those who compulsively react to physical flaws. A fixation on imperfection becomes the focus of our bodies and our surroundings, such that all that is slightly tarnished becomes a practice in purification. When we're immersed in negative self-image, crab apple offers the elixir of divine self-love through the renewal of how we perceive ourselves.

Nitpicking about a hair out of place, obsessing over a tiny blemish, or constantly tidying up, the crab apple challenge elicits self-loathing. We feel disgusted in our surroundings and in ourselves. We pick at our faults, no matter how minor or irrelevant to those around us. At the heart of the matter, we are bogged down in the mire of trying to chase after unrealistic standards of purity.

Crab apple's salvation emerges as a slow and steady sense of enhanced self-love. We begin to embrace our imperfections as part of our wholeness—not broken, but made complete through our own loving acceptance. I've witnessed the transformative effects on survivors of sexual and physical abuse, who carry an aversion to their bodies. Crab apple plays a major role in helping us release our negative self-image and adopt an attitude of self-acceptance and love, perhaps for the first time in our lives.

For decades I've worked to shift the energy of trauma and cultivate self-love, for myself as well as for helping others. Crab apple has proven to be a stalwart ally through times of tumult, when the focus is on the flaws. As I write this book, I'm recovering from a recent bout with benign skin cancer, which called for surgery on my face to remove two spots. Throughout the healing process, I added two drops of crab apple in my topical skin toner spray. As I applied the remedy to my face twice a day, I experienced a gentle transition from "freaked out" about the 2-inch surgical scar prominently displayed on my face, to *accepting* it as part of my face, and almost magically it began to heal more quickly. Interestingly, I found that the less I "obsessed," the more quickly my skin healed. This flower has taught me like no other how to let go of expectations of beauty, and to truly release the fixation on the details and finally embrace the perfect wholeness of my being. A powerful lesson I learned in working with the crab apple challenge is that when we focus our attention on and pick at the scab, we participate in its proliferation. But when we relax our gaze on our appearance, there becomes a softer glow, an authentic filter that sees the loveliness that was there all along.

OVERCARE for WELFARE of OTHERS

Chicory, Vervain, Vine, Beech, Rock Water

These are the flowers that relate to control and rigidity. Although the title might suggest wanting to do what's best for others, what Dr. Bach recognized in this grouping was a sense of tension when others are not following suit. The ways in which this shows up might be in the form of emotional manipulation (chicory), self-righteous speech (vervain), or critical judgments of others (beech). There may be a sense of being wound too tight and having to be in charge to feel at ease (vine). Sometimes you might even wish that others would follow your lead, even though you hold yourself to a standard too high for anyone to reach (rock water). The flowers in this category free you from spending time worrying about whether you are right or wrong, and whether others are good enough or not. They help you relax your grip and peacefully live and let live.

Journal Prompts for Exploring Overcare for Others

Where do I feel tension in my body?
What can I release?
What do I cherish about my partner / friends / family members?

Chicory

Cichorium intybus

I give of myself without expectations.

Challenges: possessive, clingy, codependent
Transformations: unconditional love, selfless, secure

When we observe the habit of this tenacious wild plant, we see an overbearing profusion of blue flowers. Wiry stems intertwine around anything that grows nearby, gripping for dear life. There's an emotional insecurity displayed in the chicory type's codependent clinginess. Think of the older parent who coerces with gifts, so that the adult child will visit. Or the overly attached friend who runs a guilt trip when we spend time with other friends.

The challenges associated with chicory flower are indeed intense. Since it's in the "overcare" category, we see this displayed as a form of smothering love. The intention may be to want to help and take care of family and friends, yet the emotional neediness oversteps boundaries, creates rifts in our relationships, and drives loved ones away.

When we begin to open to the healing energy of chicory, a sense of ease develops, and a release of inner tension, which opens a path for healthful relationships to emerge. As we learn to trust in the act of unconditional love, we strengthen our powers of selflessness, and we experience true security with our loved ones. We become more able to give of ourselves without expectations, which makes others *want* to be with us, in return.

When Nicole came to see me, she was stressed about her relationship with her longtime boyfriend, whom she lived with. She recognized that she didn't feel confident in asking for what she needed from him, so she would act clingy to get attention. Nicole recalled waiting by the window for him to come home from work on most days, then following him around the house with a barrage of comments, questions about his day, and suggestions on how they could spend time together. She felt like she was nipping at his heels like a tenacious puppy. It was exhausting for them both. We decided to include chicory in her combination remedy, and after just a short time, Nicole felt a loosening of her grip. She began to release her expectations placed on her partner, which led to a closer bond between them, devoid of codependent energy. Chicory is also a wonderful remedy for children and animals who cling to their caregivers' heels and might cry or whine to be held. The transformation is a secure way of being that flows with the energy of unconditional love.

Vervain

Verbena officinalis

I relax and allow life to unfold peacefully.

Challenges: overly enthusiastic, self-righteous, tense
Transformations: open-minded, thoughtful, calm

Vervain stems have a sturdy wiriness that show the tenacity of this prolific plant and can be compared with the overbearing quality that is displayed in the vervain character's challenge. Imagine a religious evangelist on a podium, fervently spouting their fixed views, perhaps pounding a fist, and creating a dramatic display of emotion. Or maybe when checking your social media you're met with a barrage of emphatic, self-righteous posts, crying their cause. Whether it's religious fanaticism or zealous admonishment, the vervain type can be heard passionately exercising their voice.

A keynote of this remedy is overly enthusiastic speech, which can be seen as a form of control through persuasive language.

A lawyer who argues their case and won't back down is yet another example of this challenging state. Those in need of vervain are boisterous and certain of their stance. This is a high-strung person, who takes every chance to make their point heard.

The transformation is a calm persona that engenders friendliness instead of fanaticism. As vervain flower does its work, we feel a sense of inner tension melting away, and the need to be right receding into the background. It is through this shift toward gentleness that we learn to trust ourselves and release our need to be right. In this way, we can take part in more-open and more-relaxed conversations.

One of my first coaching clients was Sonia. When she came to see me, she was suffering from MS and experienced so much pain that she couldn't get out of bed most days. We worked together for six months, and as we went deeper into the emotional correlations of her physical pain, she recognized that she would have flare-ups when she was stressed. She noticed that much of her stress came from a desire to control her environment by telling others what they should do and how they should do it. Sonia realized that she was spending much of her energy, every day, emphatically trying to convince her housemates of how things should be done. As we delved deeper into her story, she talked about losing her job right before her illness set in, and how this loss made her perceive herself as powerless. Her feelings of helplessness came to the fore as we unpacked her habit of trying to verbally persuade others to reclaim her power. As Sonia let go of her idealism and more easily embraced varied viewpoints, she held less pain in her body. The role that vervain played in helping her become more open minded was a crucial step in her healing, and a profound teaching for me on the potent medicine of this flower.

Vine

Vitis vinifera

As I relinquish control, I find freedom within.

Challenges: dominance, control, intensity
Transformations: leadership, cooperation, humility

I spent many years living in Northern California's wine country, surrounded by vine. What is most striking about the habit of this plant is the stalk's ability to twist and wrap itself around fences, trees, and other nearby plants. Although kept in neat rows and cultivated for the grapes, the vine itself behaves like a weed. It can be seen everywhere, cascading over houses, creeping up from under decks, tenaciously gripping to whatever it can take hold of.

Control in all forms is how the vine challenge shows up. Authority as displayed in the dictator who rules with an iron fist, insisting that others do things his way. There's an intensity present that manifests as force, such that others fear the wrath of vine dominance should they fail to follow orders. In its most extreme state, vine can be seen in abusive relationships, as with emotional and physical violence.

Once the remedy begins to create a shift, a softening occurs in the form of greater respect for those around us. With a new-found sense of humility, we become better able to cooperate with others. As control is relinquished, a natural ability to lead comes forth. It is within this release that the vine personality can realize true power and find freedom within.

Sometimes the vine temperament can be subtle. Natalie came to see me to work on managing her anxious feelings. She was aware of her need for organization in her home, and how she felt uneasy when others didn't follow her orders. Often, she was frustrated with her housemates and found herself constantly dictating as to where things should go, and how the house rules should be governed. This was problematic for her housemates, but mostly it was terrible for Natalie. She suffered much, trying to control her surroundings all the time. We worked together for several months before I recognized this as a vine challenge. You see, Natalie was soft spoken and unassuming, a kind and rational community member; she didn't possess the typical domineering stance as seen in the vine demeanor. As we unpacked her stress around a need to control everything around her, vine became clear. This remedy was transformational in helping Natalie let go and practice strong leadership, devoid of dominance.

Fagus sylvatica

I release judgment and welcome the ways of others.

Challenges: judgment, irritability, intolerance
Transformations: empathy, tolerance, kindness

One of the more familiar challenges that we can each relate to at one time or another is that of feeling irritated or annoyed by the ways of others. Like an itchy rash on the inside, the beech challenge emerges from within and comes out through the mode of intolerance. When I sit with someone and they talk constantly about how much so-and-so annoys them, or how much such-and-such irritates them, I note beech as a key remedy for their healing. An important lesson I've learned in working with these difficult feelings is that often when we're projecting judgments outward onto others, we're holding judgments inward for ourselves.

The beech challenge is seething—hiding somewhere in the depths of our experience and surprising even the best of us when condemnation arises. It can be fleeting, as with minor peeves over friends' or loved ones' less-than-perfect behaviors, or it can run deep, blocking our ability to welcome the differences of others, creating an air of animosity. There's an inner dialogue that's reactionary and keeps us stuck in a state of constant criticism.

As the remedy begins to shed light on the habit of judgment, tolerance surfaces and our heart opens with empathy. There's a soothing effect as kindness comes to the fore, and we release our disapproval for what others do. Through this lens of acceptance, we no longer feel consumed by judgment, and we're able to fully embrace the unique temperament and qualities that each being possesses.

Kelly was a young woman whom I worked with to help her manage family trauma. Together, we uncovered many layers of emotional challenge, and one that stood out as significant for her was that of extreme judgment toward others. Often, Kelly found herself annoyed by her friends and irritated by her co-workers. This became a problem for her, since she began losing friends and couldn't stick with a job because of her intense perceptions. Kelly was aware of how these reactions felt terrible in her body, and over the course of several weeks she worked with beech to address her critical views and to soften her constant judgments about others, which ultimately led her to look at and transform the ways in which she harshly judged herself.

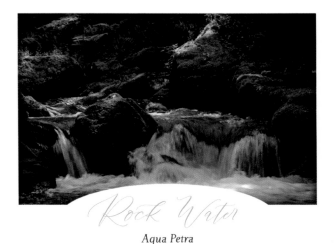

Rock Water

Aqua Petra

I release rigidity as I receive flexibility.

Challenges: rigidity, high standards, self-denial
Transformations: flexibility, adaptability, joy

Rock water is the only remedy in the system that does not come from a plant but is water that was originally made by Dr. Bach from a pristine, ancient spring in Wales. When we imagine water flowing effortlessly from primordial rock, we can begin to embody the cleansing properties at work. A soul renewal as we become better able to relax into our authentic rhythms, devoid of rigidity. In this way, we succumb to our natural flow, release our too-high ideals, and learn to enjoy life more fully.

The primary indication of the rock water challenge is that of holding oneself to unreasonably high standards. "Perfectionist"—a self-label that I hear from those who adhere to such a level. Those in need of this remedy are overachievers who will sacrifice their own happiness to accomplish all they set out to reach. The challenge is exacerbated when they hold others to these lofty heights, by way of setting a "stellar" example. These are not vocal types, who *tell* others what to do; rather, they *expect* others to follow their impeccable lead without being told.

When reflecting on the properties of water, Dr. Bach stated, "Nothing is more flexible than water, yet nothing can resist it." Which speaks to the defiance of flow. The transformation that rock water brings is a softening of strict standards, which allows for flexibility—an ability to touch joy and surrender to spontaneity. Once this sense of tenderness is activated within, we can continue our good work with greater ease and have more fun along the way.

A few years ago, my family and I were hiking in the Anza Borrego Desert. It's a magical place with bighorn sheep, and rare wildflowers adorning the trails. As we descended the canyon in the 90-degree heat, we came upon a waterfall with a shallow pool. Right away, my daughter and husband stripped down and waded into the crystal-clear water. At first I was hesitant, but then I gave in and rolled up my pants and splashed around. To do something just for the sake of fun is a lesson I've been tested with my entire life. Now, here I was, with nothing to do but allow for the flow of joy. Then it struck me . . . I was immersed in a pool of rock water! As I relaxed into the coolness, I looked down and spotted a mama frog with her baby on her back, playfully floating along. I laughed, since their presence reminded me that play is an essential part of life, and to experience joy is our inherent nature. Frisking in the cool waters without an agenda and allowing the bliss to wash over me was truly a rock water healing.

Water, the last remedy in Dr. Bach's system, feels relevant in our cultivation of a deeper communion with nature, and in learning how to utilize the medicine available within this sacred source.

Rescue Remedy®

Cherry Plum, Clematis, Impatiens, Rock Rose, Star-of-Bethlehem

I am focused, calm, and alert.

Challenges: emergencies, acute trauma, intense emotions
Transformations: calm, inner peace, relaxation

Rescue Remedy® is the most widely used Bach flower remedy worldwide and is the only combination formula developed by Dr. Bach. What's unique about Rescue Remedy® is that it's intended to be used in acute instances of accidents or traumas of any kind. Dr. Bach found that each of these specific five flowers plays a distinctive role in addressing shock and trauma, moving one past these temporary states. Both cherry plum and rock rose relate to specific fears, the former with loss of control, and the latter with terror. Clematis works to keep one grounded in the present moment when shock takes one out of body. Impatiens keeps one calm and focused, while star-of-Bethlehem provides a sense of inner peace.

This formula can be used whenever there is an unexpected accident or extreme upset, and preventively to offset any panic or fear (such as anticipation of a doctor's appointment, hospital visit, or school exam). This powerful mixture is not intended for long-term use but should be kept on hand to be used acutely, as needed. Common uses include panic attacks, difficulty falling asleep or falling back to sleep after a nightmare, rebalancing after an accident or argument, and restoration after travel or physical stress. The dosage is four drops, as often as needed, until a sense of balance and calm is restored.

Journal Prompts for Exploring Acute Trauma

How does my body feel in this moment?
What sensations do I notice?
Where do I feel at peace in my body?

CHAPTER 3
AN ONGOING
Journey

Working with Others

Once you feel confident selecting remedies for yourself, you will likely want to share the flowers with others. When your friends and family hear about the glowing results you're having, it won't be long before someone asks you to select remedies for them. And of course, if you're a healing-arts practitioner, you'll want to incorporate flower remedies into your current practice, so that you have better outcomes. Whether you're helping a friend with a problem, supporting a loved one with a challenge, or guiding a client toward deeper healing, the method is the same. Reflecting on the current challenges together and helping the other person gain clarity around their chronic and acute emotional states is the conduit for positive change. The support of a caring guide is a foundational element of any co-creative healing process. Everyone is their own best healer, and we are there to encourage awareness and support growth by listening, then offering the flowers that correlate to the recognized emotional challenges. When I meet with clients for healing sessions, most of the time is spent with them talking about and reflecting on their feelings. I steer clear of talking about past experiences and physical symptoms and focus on what is *currently* up for them. Of course, they can share as much as they wish, but *it is not necessary to know about past trauma to heal!* This is a big revelation for many and helps ease the process, since the past feels less daunting when we're grounded in the here and now.

Many of the women I see are mothers. Some I've known through pregnancy and birth, and we work together to select remedies for their children. I especially love working with babies. Since they can communicate only through sounds and expressions, it's fun to discern what they're feeling, and it's empowering for mothers to understand what's being conveyed. This practice alone is supportive, in that the mother reflects on what the child is feeling, and, in this way, honors the challenge, which fills the emotional need. Not trying to "fix" what's wrong but offering an energy medicine ally to comfort and soothe. It's always rewarding to hear back from a mother as she tells me that the challenge has subsided. This shows the efficacy of flower remedies, whether the person is aware of taking them or not.

This leads to a question I get often: "Can I dose a loved one with flowers without them knowing?" The answer is that you *can*, but what does it say about the relationship if you don't feel you can tell them that they might benefit from a flower ally? Understandably, it can get touchy when we see the challenges of our loved ones more clearly than they do. Yet another beautiful aspect of flower therapy is that it's easier to relate a universal emotional challenge through the archetype of a flower description, rather than telling your loved one that they talk about themselves too much and perhaps could practice listening more to others. That said, the remedy will indeed work whether a person knows they're taking it or not if it's the right flower for the underlying cause.

Working with Animals

One of my favorite ways to work with flower remedies is to help animals move through emotional blockages. Since we can't communicate with animals verbally, it's best to explore one essence at a time and watch the behaviors for any changes. Animals are sensitive beings and respond to subtle energy quickly. Often only one or two doses of a single remedy is needed to resolve acute challenges.

A notable experience of this was when my young daughter was riding her horse on a woodland trail and the horse stepped on a wasp's nest. Both were stung many times, and the horse threw my daughter off and ran into the woods. They made it safely back home, and both were given Rescue Remedy® for a couple of days. The next week when my daughter went to ride, the horse stopped every time they came to a gate. We remembered that the wasp incident happened near a gate in the woods, and the horse seemed to associate this with the traumatic event. She was clearly afraid to go any farther. Knowing what had happened, I gave her single remedy of mimulus, which relates to fear with a known cause. Two drops in her drinking water several times a day for a few days cured her of this fear, and she was able to move past gates as if nothing had happened.

Some Useful Flowers for Animals:

Crab apple—obsessive cleansing or grooming
Mimulus—Fear with a known cause
Vervain, heather, or chicory—excessive barking or whining;
  "vocalizing"; clinginess
Vine—dominance, bullying, "alpha dog"
Star-of-Bethlehem—trauma, past or present
Walnut—difficulty adapting to change
Rescue Remedy®—any acute intense experiences

For acute challenges, the dosage is two drops of a single remedy or four drops of a combination formula (or Rescue Remedy®) in the animal's drinking water for a few days. For smaller animals, you can create a dosage bottle, without alcohol, and give four drops from here, to minimize the amount of alcohol used. For chronic challenges, typically a few weeks of taking the remedy will provide a change in behavior. Once the desired shift has taken place, discontinue use.

Working with Plants

Yes, you can use flower remedies to help plants to thrive as well! Once, I had a greenhouse in Northern California where I grew roses. I tended them every day, and they grew to be over 6 feet tall, with deliciously fragrant blooms. One day, I noticed an aphid infestation on one of the bushes. Sticky white bugs clung to the stems and enveloped the buds, trying to suffocate the life out of the plant. I added four drops of Rescue Remedy® and two drops of crab apple to a spray bottle and sprayed around the base of the soil and on the leaves. I applied this mixture twice a day for about a week, and each day the infestation lessened, until the bugs were gone.

Here are a few key remedies that relate to common plant challenges:

Crab apple for any disease or insect infestation

Walnut for plants that have been moved or cut back, to help them adjust to the change

Star-of-Bethlehem for shock and trauma, such as frost, extreme heat, or a critter attack

Dosage:
Add several drops of each chosen flower to the base of the plant, four times per day. You can also add the drops to a spray bottle of spring water and apply several squirts directly to the soil and on the leaves.

Rescue Remedy® can be used for any signs of trauma or shock.

Use until the plant is recovered.

Flower Remedies for Topical Use

When we perceive something as "wrong" with our physical appearance or a discomfort to our bodies, this causes us to have a distorted self-image and halts the healing process as we become discouraged or disgusted. It is indeed called for to use the corresponding remedies internally, and you can also use the remedies topically to address the emotional challenges that accompany hair and skin symptoms. In this way, you absorb the positive energy of the flowers through the receptive cells of your skin and hair, which creates a greater sense of nourishment, comfort, and inner balance.

Aging skin, thinning hair, acne, eczema, poison oak, and shingles are some common challenges related to physical appearance. Flower remedies are used topically by adding several drops of a single flower or combination formula to your skin and hair products or your bath water.

Here are a few of my favorite flowers that address common emotional states related to appearance:

Crab apple is the best remedy when there are feelings of disgust or impurity. One might have a habit of fixating on minor blemishes or imperfections. This flower helps impart self-acceptance of physical appearance and a positive body image.

Gentian is the remedy of choice when one is discouraged after a setback. Perhaps there was a sudden outbreak of acne or loss of hair due to hormonal shifts or stress, and one feels unsure that they will recover. This flower provides courage and an ability to forge ahead in the face of doubt and despondency and to gain trust in the healing process.

Honeysuckle is used when there is a sense of melancholy relating to the past. When one is preoccupied with wanting to return to a more youthful time, this remedy helps one accept their present experience and embrace the aging process with grace and ease.

Impatiens, as its name suggests, is used when there are feelings of impatience and anxiousness around physical appearance. Those in need are annoyed by the time that it takes the body to heal. This flower helps soothe irritation and provides feelings of calm and tolerance.

Walnut is used for adapting to any sudden changes with our appearance, at any stage of life. This flower allows for smooth transitions as well as protection from external influences such as environmental toxins that show up in the hair and skin.

How to Make a Flower Remedy Mother Tincture

Making a flower remedy is a wonderful opportunity for communing with nature, and it's fun. Observing the creative elements at play is a spiritually satisfying process, which attunes you to your soul connection to flowers. Although purchasing high-quality remedies from trusted sources is the best way to begin practicing the art of flower therapy, (see "Resources" section for where to purchase), I always encourage students to make a flower remedy from scratch, using the "sunlight method," at least once a year. This artful practice is a deeply inspiring activity and can be done on any given sunny day. You can use any plant in full bloom that appeals to you, regardless of its indications for use or lack thereof. In other words, it doesn't matter if the flower is already a remedy with known properties or not. The practice is to deeply connect with the flower energy, to witness the alchemy. In this way you become more aware of and grounded in the complete process. It's like growing your own tomatoes and the thrill of seeing them go from seed to fruit, versus buying a ripe tomato from the market. Although a ripe tomato may be delicious, you don't get the opportunity to witness the extraordinary process of fruition.

Attending to a flower while its energy is potentized by the sun and captured by the water is mesmerizing. I relate the first time I made a remedy as a class homework assignment, with an excerpt from my notebook: "When the clouds parted to reveal a blue, sunny sky, I cut two stalks from the plant. As soon as I placed the flowers in the bowl of water, I was transfixed. The luminescent quality of the flowers showed through the glass, displaying shades of lavender, pale blue, and creamy greenish white, aglow in the sunlight. Within the first few minutes, the alchemical process is apparent. The flowers bond with the water, which is catalyzed by the sunlight, creating a sparkling effect. The slight breeze gently stirs the petals, as the flowers seem at peace. I have work to do inside, but I don't want to leave and miss any of this magical process."

Summer is the ultimate season for making flower remedies, with long days of unadulterated sunshine. When I wake up and the sun is at its brightest, with clear blue skies, I wander through the garden to see what's in bloom.

What You'll Need

Small glass bowl. Sterilize ahead of time by running it through the dishwasher or hand-washing it in hot water.

Purest water available—ideally fresh from a local spring, or spring water sold in a glass bottle

Garden shears or scissors

Small tea or hand strainer

Glass measuring cup

4 oz. dark glass dropper bottle

Small funnel

Alcohol spirits to preserve the remedy. Traditionally, grape brandy is used, but any spirits will do.

What to Do

Choose a flowering plant that has fresh, vibrant blooms. Some common Bach flowers that are found blooming throughout many parts of North America and Europe in spring and summer are white chestnut, agrimony, chicory, and wild rose.

Place the glass bowl in direct sunlight, as close to the plant as possible. Make sure that shadows won't fall across the bowl for the next three to four hours.

Fill the bowl with spring water, leaving some room for the flowers.

Snip the flowers and let them drop into the bowl, being careful not to touch them. Gently guide them into the water with the shears.

Once the surface is full of the freshest blooms, top off the bowl with water.

Let the decoction sit in the sun for three to four hours, until the flowers look like they're beginning to wilt.

Preserving the Mother Tincture

When the time is up, use a stick from the plant to gently lift the flowers out of the bowl. Be careful not to touch the water with your hands.

Pour the liquid into the measuring cup, using the strainer to filter out any plant material and debris.

You will be left with a measuring cup of pure flower remedy—the "mother tincture." I like to use a clean glass dropper to taste a few drops of the tincture before it's preserved, since each one has a unique, subtle flavor.

Transfer 2 oz. of the tincture to the 4 oz. glass bottle, filling it halfway.

Fill the remainder of the bottle with 2 oz. of alcohol spirits as the preservative.

Label the bottle with the name of the flower "mother tincture," date, place, and whom it was prepared by. It will keep stored in a cool, dark place, indefinitely.

I like to feed the leftover unpreserved remedy to the plant that was used, to nourish the flow of life force energy.

The dosage of a single remedy is always two drops, taken alone or added to a combination formula. With this ratio in mind, you can make many subsequent stock-bottle remedies from just two drops of the mother tincture, and you can make many dosage bottles from just two drops of the stock remedy.

Creating a Stock Bottle from the Mother Tincture

When you purchase a flower remedy, what you get is the "stock bottle." This is what you use to create combination formulas or use in acute instances, directly from the bottle.

Add two drops of the mother tincture to a 1 oz. dropper bottle filled half with spring water and half with alcohol spirits. That's all!

Label the bottle with the name of the flower remedy and date. Since it's preserved with full-strength alcohol, the shelf life of a stock bottle is indefinite, although the brandy may begin to taste "off" within five years or so.

Creating a Dosage Bottle from a Stock Bottle

Add two drops of the flower remedy from the stock bottle to a 1 oz. dropper bottle filled with spring water and a couple of droppers of alcohol spirits.

After your flower remedy is made, you can "play with" the energy by taking it internally, over the course of one or two months, and listening for the messages that call to be heard. Keep a notebook to observe any shifts in awareness or changes in habits that feel related to the energy of the flower. If it's a Bach flower, you can compare your experiences with the indications for use. This is a wonderful way to learn more about the healing properties of the flower, firsthand. If it's a flower from your garden or that you found on the hiking trail, you can feel into the energy by reflecting on your insights and recognizing the support provided for you.

Continuing Your Flower Therapy Studies

Engaging with the art of flower therapy is an ongoing exploration. Each time I teach a class, I learn more by witnessing the shared experiences of my students. It's a truly holistic practice, since it relies on the collective wisdom of each of us to deepen and confirm our insights. Since the FDA does not provide studies on herbal and energy medicines, we must turn toward and trust our empirical experience.

The best way to deepen your understanding of flower healing is to become a practitioner. The Bach Centre in the UK is the leader on information and education regarding the thirty-eight original Bach flower remedies. Although you may practice flower therapy without any certification, the Bach Centre in the UK offers the international Bach Foundation Registered Practitioner course (BFRP) both online and in locations throughout the world. You must pass a written exam and submit client case studies to obtain your BFRP status. It takes about eighteen months to complete, and I highly recommend this rewarding course of study. Even if you don't intend to see clients, you will benefit from the deeper learning available from the immersive format. Visit www.bachcentre.com.

Patricia Kaminski and Richard Katz are the founders of the Flower Essence Society. They host educational workshops and a practitioner program annually on their biodynamic farm, Terra Flora, in Northern California. They offer a yearly membership that gives you access to their online repertory of over one hundred flower remedies, including the Bach flowers. They've been a trusted resource of flower remedy research, development, sales, and education since 1979. Visit www.flowersociety.org.

Flower therapy and self-improvement courses at Dina Saalisi Healing Arts are founded in the belief that we are all healers at the core, and that an active connection with the energies of nature is our greatest source of support and empowerment. In helping others deepen awareness of their emotional landscape and activate their skills of inner healing, I lead classes and workshops, online and in person. Visit www.dinasaalisi.com.

Listen to flowers! To continue to learn about the deep healing available from nature, practice communing with flower energy regularly. Prioritize a weekly trail hike or visit to a botanical garden and grow flowers in your backyard. Keep a dedicated unlined journal to write about and sketch your encounters with the flowers that call to you. From this connection, you create a more empowered way of being that carries you forward on your path to heal, thrive, and live a vibrant life.

RESOURCES

Bach Flower Indications by Category

Fear

Rock rose—extreme fear, terror; nightmares
Mimulus—fears that can be named, nervousness, timidity
Cherry plum—fear of losing control, irrational thoughts, impulsiveness
Aspen—fear without reason; uneasiness; apprehension
Red chestnut—fear and worry about loved ones

Uncertainty

Cerato—inability to trust inner knowing; seeking answers from outside sources
Scleranthus—indecisive, difficulty choosing between two things, wavering
Gentian—discouragement after a setback; disappointment; lack of faith
Gorse—hopelessness, doubt, negativity

Hornbeam—mental exhaustion, procrastination, lack of focus
Wild oat—lack of direction; confusion about life path

Not Sufficient Interest in Present Circumstances

Clematis—inability to focus, dreamy, clumsy
Honeysuckle—longing for the past; melancholy;
    homesickness
Wild rose—apathy, disinterest in life, boredom
Olive—exhaustion, depletion, difficulty recovering from
    illness
White chestnut—overthinking, worry, rumination
Mustard—sadness for no apparent reason, gloom
Chestnut bud—inability to learn from mistakes; repeating
    old patterns; difficulty retaining information

Loneliness

Water violet—aloof, introverted, isolated
Impatiens—impatient, anxious, living in the future
Heather—overtalkative, self-obsessed, clingy

Oversensitive to Influences & Ideas

Agrimony—hides true feelings behind a facade; inner
    turmoil
Centaury—weak will, subservience, self-sacrifice
Walnut—difficulty adjusting to change, vulnerable, easily
    swayed
Holly—jealousy, hatred, spite

Despondency or Despair

Larch—lack of confidence, repressed self-expression
Pine—guilt, shame, self-judgment
Elm—overwhelm, stress, burden
Sweet chestnut—anguish, darkness, despair
Star-of-Bethlehem—shock, trauma, grief
Willow—resentment, bitterness, blame
Oak—overworked, inability to rest, dutiful
Crab apple—negative self-image, lack of self-love, fixation on flaws

Overcare for Welfare of Others

Chicory—possessive, clingy, codependent
Vervain—overly enthusiastic; self-righteous; tense
Vine—dominance, control, intensity
Beech—judgment, irritability, intolerance
Rock water—rigidity, high standards, self-denial

Rescue Remedy®

Cherry plum, clematis, impatiens, rock rose, star-of-Bethlehem—emergencies, acute trauma, intense emotions

Where to Purchase Flower Remedies

The Bach flower remedies can be found in natural food stores, herbal apothecaries, and holistic pharmacies worldwide and online. Check with your local shops to see if they carry them, or request that they order them for you.

You can purchase the original Bach flower remedies directly from the Bach Centre in the UK. They ship internationally. www.bachcentre.com/en/shop/

The Flower Essence Society has an online store where you can purchase individual remedies and kits. I recommend their "Healing Herbs" kit of the thirty-eight Bach flowers, which is made in the UK by Julian Barnard. It doesn't boast the "Bach" brand but is tried and true nonetheless and ships directly from Northern California. www.fesflowers.com

BIBLIOGRAPHY

Bach, Edward. *The Essential Writings of Dr. Edward Bach: The Twelve Healers and Heal Thyself*. London: Vermilion, 2005.

Ball, Stefan. *Bloom*. London: Vermilion, 2006.

Ball, Stefan, and Judy Ramsell-Howard. *Bach Flower Remedies for Animals: The Definitive Guide to Treating Animals with the Bach Remedies*. London: Vermilion, 2005.

Barnard, Julian. *Bach Flower Remedies: The Essence Within*. London: Winter, 2010.

Kaminski, Patricia. *Flowers That Heal: How to Use Flower Essences*. Dublin, Ireland: Newleaf, 1998.

Ramsell-Howard, Judy. *The Bach Flower Remedies Step by Step: A Complete Guide to Using and Selecting the Remedies*. London: Random House, 2005.

Scheffer, Mechthild. *Bach Flower Therapy: Theory and Practice*. Wellingborough, UK: Thorsons, 1986.

Index
of the Thirty-Eight
BACH FLOWERS

Dina Saalisi

Dina Saalisi is a holistic healer with skills as a master flower essence practitioner, board-certified health-and-wellness coach, certified hypnotherapist, educator, and empath. An energeticist with an extraordinary gift for connecting with the many facets of life force energy, her system of healing is grounded in reverence for nature and the nourishment provided from this universal source. By combining these powerful healing methods, Dina guides others in creating personal empowerment to overcome physical and emotional challenges at the core. She lives in California with her family and two pups, where she can be found listening to flowers amid the many hiking trails, gardens, and parks. http://dinasaalisi.com